D1244949

Green Light Fundraising:

Your Sustainable Fundraising Guide to Raising $50,000 to $500,000 a Year to Light Up the Eyes of People You Serve and Your Donors

By Rich Foss

Evergreen Leaders
19235 Plow Creek Rd.
Tiskilwa, IL 61368

Evergreen Leaders paperback edition published February 2012

Visit us at: http://greenlightfundraising.org or http://evergreenleaders.org
Designed by Jason Clough and Bryn Hovde.

Printed by Entrust Source.

Foss, Rich.
Greenlight Fundraising: Your Sustainable Fundraising Guide to Raising $50,000 to $500,000 a Year to Light Up the Eyes of People You Serve and Your Donors / by Rich Foss

1. Fund raising. 2: Corporations, Nonprofit--Finance 3. Title

ISBN-10: 098510922X

ISBN-13: 978-0-9851092-2-6

For all the people helped by nonprofits I've raised money for and whose courage and transformed lives continue to inspire.

For my grandchildren: Aaliyah, Langston, Yakim, and Nadia.

And for my wife Sarah who continues to dazzle me with her organizational genius and her ability to make life sweet.

Green Light Fundraising

Foreword by Marc A. Pitman. *Author of Ask Without Fear!*

Have you noticed that as we move into the 21st century, fundraising isn't getting any easier? The good news is that despite the economy, it isn't really getting any harder. Especially if you follow advice like the kind found in this book.

Rich Foss has done a terrific job of combining excellent fundraising practices with both his real-life experience and the experience of his clients. Green Light Fundraising is packed full of compelling stories, insightful questions, practical tools, and realistic timetables. He covers everything from researching a campaign to marketing it—even using social media—to assembling teams and making asks. He's absolutely right that the best way to fundraise is face-to-face solicitations. But he even includes great information on holding successful events and direct mail appeals. And I love his repeated reminder to celebrate and thank—two things nonprofits regularly forget.

As a person who shares Rich's passion for nonprofits, I like the fact that he offers creative ways nonprofits can access help over and above the thorough guidance given in the book.

If you want to get off of the special events treadmill, get a copy of this book. But make sure you have a pen and some paper handy. I've been at fundraising for a long-time and I was taking notes!

To your fundraising success,

Marc A. Pitman, CFCC

FundraisingCoach.com and author of *Ask Without Fear!*

INTRODUCTION

You are reading this book because a nonprofit you care about needs to jump-start its ability to raise more money. You may be the development director, the executive director, or a board member and you are checking this book because you are looking for a better way to raise money.

At the same time you are most likely scared because you don't know how to go about it. Perhaps your nonprofit has done some special events, perhaps a holiday appeal letter, but you need to raise a lot more money.

That's the situation Dave McClure, executive director of the Youth Service Bureau of Illinois Valley, was in. In thirty years of serving troubled youth and families, the most money YSB had raised in a single year from individuals and businesses was $7800.

I taught Dave the system you will find outlined in this book and they raised way more money than he could imagine.

As part of teaching the system to Dave, I taught him the power of stories to convey to volunteers and potential donors the work of his nonprofit.

One day I received a call from Dave. "Rich," he said, "you won't believe what just happened. Remember that story I told this morning at the campaign steering committee about the grandmother who was worried about the safety of her young grandson? He was living with his mother in a house with several other adults who were into drugs."

I remembered. The grandmother had talked to Dave a few days before and, after listening to her story, Dave had said that YSB had a program designed to provide support and teaching to young mothers on how to be good parents. This program could help the young mother move into a safer environment and learn to care for her son better.

Unfortunately, YSB has limited funding for the program and we will not be able to enroll the young mother and son until another young mother completed it, Dave told the campaign steering committee after recounting his conversation with the grandmother.

On the phone Dave said, "One of the people at the campaign steering committee just called to tell me that she wants to donate the lead gift of $10,000 and have it used to help this woman's daughter and grandson."

Need More Help From Rich? See p. 241

GREEN LIGHT
FUNDRAISING

In that $10,000 gift, YSB raised more money through one gift than it had in all gifts combined for any previous year.

Dave and the YSB staff members were geniuses at juggling government funding from as many as 53 federal, state, and local sources. Of course, every year or so, one of the governmental funding sources dropped out of the picture and they were scrambling to find funding for one essential program after another. Their board of directors had been encouraging Dave, YSB's longtime executive director, to build a fundraising base to add to the mix of governmental funding sources.

That's when Dave contacted me and we began the process outlined in this book—developing a sustainable fundraising program that YSB could depend on year after year. In the first year, YSB went from raising $7800 to over $60,000.

Why had YSB waited for so many years to develop a fundraising program?

Fundraising is intimidating. No executive director or board member became a nonprofit leader because of a love of fundraising. People become nonprofit leaders because they are passionate about changing the lives of a specific group of people or a specific place on our planet, and a nonprofit seems like a good way to make the change happen.

YSB needed to learn the skills and to set up the systems that sustain and grow its fundraising efforts year after year.

This book is designed to help you do the same thing—to help learn the tools and to set up the systems that sustain and grow your fundraising efforts year after year.

GREEN LIGHT
FUNDRAISING

Step by step you will learn to:

1. Set your fundraising goal;
2. Create smart and friendly systems that help your campaign to grow and sustain your organization year after year;
3. Move your volunteers, donors, and community through the powerful stories of how your nonprofit transforms lives;
4. Engage your inner circle of board and staff to give every year;
5. Use a burnout-free system of recruiting enthusiastic volunteer leaders;
6. Recruit teams of volunteers who raise an amazing amount of money;
7. Teach your volunteers the GOOD way of asking for gifts;
8. Celebrate each campaign milestone.

Why affordable?

Why does Evergreen Leaders give away a lot of information and focus on making its sustainable fundraising programs affordable?

Along with eight friends, I founded the nonprofit, Evergreen Leaders, in 2003, because I passionately believe in the work of nonprofits.

I have spent a thirty-year career as a nonprofit leader and fundraiser. While helping nonprofits raise over $4 million, I have seen over and over again the incredible work that nonprofits do in our communities.

At the same time I've seen nonprofit leaders get lost trying to attract funding, supervise staff and volunteers, build strong organizations, hire talented staff, get work done, and plan for the future.

In the recent deep economic recession, I've listened to nonprofit leaders agonize over cutting staff. One CEO said to me, "I feel like the organization is a diabetic patient. First, I had to amputate the foot. Now it looks like I am going to have to amputate above the knee."

GREEN LIGHT
FUNDRAISING

Evergreen Leaders is a nonprofit with the mission to give other nonprofits money and leadership tools to transform lives.

We are constantly trying to discover new ways of giving tools to our clients and to the nonprofit world to reduce consulting costs and increase the amount of funds that go directly to transforming the lives of the people each nonprofit serves.

Since this book is long for a typical e-book, we are providing this paperback as an affordable alternative to the free e-book. While the principles of sustainable fundraising have a tradition in successful fundraising, technology is affecting both fundraising and the training of fundraisers. Help us improve. At the end of every chapter is an e-mail address (comment@greenlightfundraising.org) devoted to improving our information products. When something is unclear, or you have a suggestion for improving the book, e-mail us. If applicable, please identify the page and paragraph. Or you may have a story from your nonprofit that illustrates a point in the book. We'd love to hear from you. If we use your suggestion, you'll be added to the list of contributors at the end of the book.

One of the pleasures of doing fundraising consulting is seeing how clients creatively adapt the skills and systems we teach to their own setting. Please feel free to adapt this book to your nonprofit.

Let us know how it's working for you. We want to celebrate with you.

Note

In certain sections of the book I refer to the role and tasks of the director of development. Depending on the size of your organization, you may not have a director of development. In that case, the role and tasks of the director of development can be carried out by a volunteer, an intern, a board member, the executive director, or a combination of the above.

This book contains a clear set of instructions for carrying out a Green Light Fundraising campaign. At the same time you will have to adapt the instructions to the circumstances of your particular nonprofit.

GREEN LIGHT
FUNDRAISING

Need more help?

Even with the help of this book, you may find it challenging to implement Green Light Fundraising.

We've created a low-cost way for you to find ongoing help while you learn sustainable fundraising. For a fee of $29 a month, you can sign up for the Green Light Fundraising Club.

Sign up today and you will gain access to the Club membership section of our website that provides you with additional resources. The Green Light Fundraising Club will provide you access to:

- The Green Light Fundraising leadership modules;
- Coaching calls with Rich covering all aspects of sustainable fundraising where you can ask your sustainable fundraising questions
- Expert interviews on specific issues in sustainable fundraising
- Podcasts of coaching calls and expert interviews
- Video tutorials on key parts of sustainable fundraising

Enjoy all the learning you will do as you read this book and, if you need further help to apply the ideas and principles in the book to your nonprofit, sign up today for the Green Light Fundraising Club.

Now it's time to dive into learning the Green Light Fundraising system. Learn it and you too can raise more money for your nonprofit than you thought possible.

Page 6

Need More Help From Rich? See p. 241

GREEN LIGHT
FUNDRAISING

CHAPTER 1

Ten Reasons to do Green Light Fundrasing

When I began my career in fundraising in 1983, I worked for an organization that focused on special events, an annual Christmas appeal, and planned giving. We were the most highly visible nonprofit in the communities we served.

We were very successful in all three areas of fundraising. At least, I thought we were until I began to look at the numbers. To be successful, we invested an incredible amount of staff time in the special events. Plus, of course, each special event had costs above and beyond staff time. The gross amount we raised looked good. The net amount we raised did not look so good.

I began to search for a better way.

In 1995 the seed that germinated into sustainable fundraising (note: I use "sustainable fundraising" and "Green Light Fundraising" as synonyms) and this book, was planted in a conversation in a conference room of a small city nonprofit. Like most community-based nonprofits, we were trying to save money.

The nonprofit needed to do its first-ever capital campaign to make it possible for seventy-six developmentally disabled adults to move from a nursing home, where they had no business living, to small group homes where life would be much better for them.

The organization needed to raise $1.2 million for the project. The executive director and I interviewed three capital campaign firms based in Chicago. The board looked at the cost of a feasibility study and said, "We'll do this campaign without a consultant."

That's how I ended up in our conference room talking to Bill Glenn, a retired YMCA exec who had directed 30-40 capital campaigns over the course of his career. He volunteered to help us on one condition.

He was frustrated with the fact that fundraising firms were taking 10-15% of the money raised in campaigns. He would help us raise $1.2 million if, after the campaign, I would write a book on how to do a capital campaign.

In 1993, I published a novel, *Jonas and Sally*. Writing a book about capital campaigns sounded like a great idea. Then reality intervened. Directing the campaign was overwhelming, even with Bill mentoring me. When we completed the campaign,

GREEN LIGHT
FUNDRAISING

raising the $1.2 million, I had made so many mistakes that I considered meeting our goal an act of God.

"Bill," I said, "now that I've directed a campaign, I realize how complex they are. I can't imagine someone being able to read a book and then lead a successful campaign."

"Oh, no," he said, "you'd have to start a business."

I wasn't interested in starting a fundraising business. Writing novels sounded a lot more fun to me.

However, a few years later, when a few friends and I founded Evergreen Leaders, a nonprofit leadership development organization, something interesting happened. Clients kept asking for help with fundraising.

As I began to work with clients, it gave me an opportunity to create the better way of fundraising that I had been searching for. I've seen organizations raise an amazing amount of money year after year once they adopted sustainable fundraising. Even during the darkest days of the recession that began in late 2008, organizations that had adopted the Green Light Fundraising model raised more money each year.

Here are ten reasons why Green Light Fundraising can benefit your organization and give you the "green light" to raise more funds each year.

1. Green Light Fundraising Weds a Nonprofit's Mission to Its Fundraising.

Green Light, or sustainable fundraising, is designed to develop a strong bond between the donor and the organization. Sustainable fundraising continually invites donors to connect with a nonprofit's mission and with the people whose lives are transformed by the work of the nonprofit.

Fresh out of graduate school, I took a job at a small-town nonprofit that served people with developmental disabilities, intending to stay a short while until I found a better job. I stayed for twenty years. Why? Within a few months, I had come to believe deeply in the mission of the organization.

GREEN LIGHT
FUNDRAISING

Eventually I was asked to direct a campaign to raise $1.2 million for a project critical to carrying out the organization's mission. Directing the campaign stretched me incredibly. I was sustained by the fact that a successful campaign would make life much better for the people who used our services. The mission sustained me.

When the organization moved from doing special events to launching its first sustainable fundraising campaign, the rugged founder of a local trucking firm served as the general chairperson of the campaign. Two of the people who received services from the nonprofit served with him on the campaign steering committee.

At a dinner celebrating the success of the first campaign, he received an appreciation plaque. In his acceptance speech, as he talked about the privilege of working with the two people who received services, tears appeared in his eyes.

The next year he gave the lead gift to the campaign.

Sustainable fundraising helps volunteers build powerful bonds with an organization and its mission.

2. Green Light Fundraising Sets Your Nonprofit's Fundraising Apart.

Your mission sets you apart. Your sustainable fundraising will also.

Because sustainable fundraising grows out of your organization's mission, you set your nonprofit apart from others who are raising funds. Every part of the campaign – from the case statement, news releases, solicitor training, to the thank you letters – highlights your organization's mission and how fundraising helps you be true to your mission.

Through sustainable fundraising, a nonprofit not only asks for money, but also tells stories of lives being transformed through the organization, thereby increasing the pool of people who are committed to the mission of the organization and available to be recruited as board members, volunteers and staff.

Need More Help From Rich? See p. 241

GREEN LIGHT
FUNDRAISING

3. Green Light Fundraising Makes It Possible to Raise 80% Through Larger Gifts and 20% Through Special Events and Direct Mail Appeals.

Many nonprofits begin their fundraising with a special event. Selling tickets to an event seems easier than asking for a donation. In my first fundraising job, I had the privilege of working with Jack Domagall, a colleague who, even though blind, was a genius at organizing special events.

Our nonprofit did everything from dinner dances to bowl-a-thons to Fifties dances. Jack always said, "We always give something to donors." The events were popular.

Unfortunately, the events were a lot of work for a little income. Another negative – people and sponsors bond to the event, not to the nonprofit.

Special events are like shampoo. You produce a great shampoo and pretty soon someone else produces a better shampoo or a cheaper shampoo and your sales go down. Our nonprofit launched the first charity golf tournament in our area. Now the summer is littered with charity golf tournaments.

Eventually, our nonprofit abandoned special events in favor of a sustainable fundraising model. Annual income from the face to face phase of the sustainable fundraising doubled in the first four years.

Despite their drawbacks, special events have a strong foothold in the nonprofit world. In Green Light Fundraising, we recommend that you consider a special event aimed at smaller donors. Chapter eighteen has tips on how to use a special event to reach smaller donors effectively.

In addition to special events, appeal letters are a great way to reach smaller donors. A well-written appeal letter allows you to tell a moving story and move supporters to make a gift to your nonprofit.

While I suggest a ratio of 80% of your fundraising come from larger gifts and 20% from special events and direct mail, the actual ration may vary. For instance,

GREEN LIGHT
FUNDRAISING

Horizon House, had been doing a very successful Christmas mailing for nearly 20 years when it switched to sustainable fundraising. Their ratio is 60% from larger gifts and 40% from the direct mail appeal.

4. Green Light Fundraising Gives Volunteers a Chance to Showcase Their Leadership, Networking, and Creative Talents.

Organizations run on talents.

I stuck around for twenty years with my first employer, not only because I came to believe deeply in the mission of the organization, but also because the nonprofit was a great place to use my talents.

Sustainable fundraising campaigns also run on talents. Marketing volunteers can have a fun time translating the mission of a nonprofit into emotionally powerful media and media relations.

Volunteer leaders recruit a team to raise funds for a great cause and see their team produce results.

Everyone involved with the campaign gets to grow his or her personal network.

5. Green Light Fundraising Creates a Way for All of the Stakeholders of a Nonprofit to Work Toward a Common Goal.

Every organization has the potential for tension between departments. Nonprofits may have potential for tension between board and staff, managers and staff, service recipients and the organization, between media and the nonprofit, and between the community and the organization.

A well-run Green Light Fundraising campaign reminds everyone of the mission of the organization. It also creates roles for everyone to contribute to the success of the campaign. For instance, the inner circle of the organization—board and staff—are asked to give first, making it possible for volunteers, who solicit in the public phase of the campaign, to tell potential donors that those closest to the need have already given.

Need More Help From Rich? See p. 241

GREEN LIGHT
FUNDRAISING

6. Green Light Fundraising Reaches Out to Every Level of Donor.

Success depends on doing first things first, as Stephen Covey noted in *7 Habits of Highly Effective People.*

Fundraisers have long known that if you are going to raise $100,000, you need a lead gift of $10,000 to $15,000. You also need several other large gifts. The rule of thumb is you will receive 80% of your goal from 20% of your donors.

The successful sustainable fundraising campaign puts first things first. Securing the lead gift and other large gifts creates the momentum for success.

Then it's time for phone calls and a letter. Asking for certain levels of gifts through phone calls is part of the mix. And the appeal letter makes it possible for the donor who wants to support your organization with a $25 gift to do so. And an appeal letter is a great way to tell a powerful story that portrays the mission of the nonprofit.

Phone calls and a letter can bring in the last 20%, which is the difference between jubilation over a successful campaign or disappointment with a campaign that has fallen short of its goal.

7. Green Light Fundraising and Loyalty Keep on Giving.

A well-run sustainable fundraising campaign helps people keep on giving. It creates loyalty – the kind of loyalty that leads a person to be the general chairperson one year and give the lead gift the next year.

People who bond with your organization's mission through serving as sustainable campaign volunteers are not shy about asking for gifts from others and they freely encourage others to volunteer for the campaign.

GREEN LIGHT
FUNDRAISING

8. Your Organization Can Raise More Money Each Year.

Clients who implemented the Evergreen Leaders sustainable approach to fundraising increased their 2009 donations by 6-17% over 2008, despite the recession.

9. Your Organization Will Learn How to Do a Capital Campaign (Without Really Trying).

An organization's first capital campaign requires significant organizational learning. Sustainable fundraising helps an organization learn many necessary skills, since it uses many of the same approaches as a capital campaign, only it's a lot less intimidating because each year's goal is significantly less than a capital campaign goal.

As you do sustainable fundraising, you are learning to recruit a campaign chairperson, recruit and manage volunteers, create a case statement, obtain a lead gift each year, and use many other skills essential to a capital campaign.

After a couple of sustainable fundraising campaigns, a capital campaign will be a lot less intimidating to the organization.

10. Green Light Fundraising Lays the Groundwork for Gifts Through Wills, Trusts, and Other Estate Gifts.

When your donor sits down with her attorney to develop an estate plan, you want her to think of your nonprofit. When every year people hear the stories of how your organization transforms the lives of people in your community, and respond by giving generously to your sustainable campaign, they bond with your organization.

People who bond deeply with your organization are more likely to remember your nonprofit in their will or trust.

We've just listed ten good reasons to make sustainable fundraising the foundation of your nonprofit's approach to fundraising. At the same time, we won't kid you; sustainable fundraising is a lot of hard work, uncertainty, and rewards.

Need More Help From Rich? See p. 241

GREEN LIGHT FUNDRAISING

Looking Ahead

You just learned ten reasons to do sustainable fundraising. Now it's time to wade into the principle of Green Light Fundraising. These principles—rules of the road—have been developed over a several-year period as I've taught nonprofits to do sustainable fundraising. Some of them are original to me and some are "borrowed" from people who have plowed the fundraising field before me.

Learn the rules in the next chapter because they'll be woven throughout the rest of the book.

How can we improve?

E-mail us at (comment@greenlightfundraising.org) to let us know when something is unclear, or you have a suggestion for improving the book. Please identify the page and paragraph that needs improving.

GREEN LIGHT
FUNDRAISING

CHAPTER 2

Your Quick Guide to the Rules of the Road for
Green Light Fundraising

The first time I directed a capital campaign was terrifying. Terrifying because we had set a goal of raising $1.2 million and the most the organization had ever raised previously in a year was $100,000. It was terrifying because the dream of a better life for 70 plus people was resting on my shoulders. It was terrifying because I had so much to learn to be able to pull off a successful campaign.

By the end of the campaign my terror had given way to a sense that this was a great learning experience. I may have learned more in those three years than any other three years in my professional career.

Through this book, you are the beneficiary of the learning I did during that campaign. Later, when I began consulting with other organizations, and began to teach them to do sustainable fundraising, I began to realize that I was teaching the same principles over and over again. These principles are the sign posts to directing a campaign.

When you take a drivers' education course, you learn the signs that tell you when to yield and when to stop. You also learn signs that warn you that a railroad crossing is ahead and tell you the speed limit. After you have driven you don't even have to think about the signs because you automatically respond to them.

It's the same way with the rules of the road for Green Light Fundraising. You will learn the rules early on and eventually they'll become second nature to you. You'll automatically apply them in your fundraising work.

The rest of this book will give you much more information on these rules of the road. Read the following rules of the road a couple times before continuing with the book and your brain will begin to assimilate them and help you later on as you study the details. Read them now and you will jump start your brain as it begins the process of making them as automatic as the rules of the road are for experienced drivers.

GREEN LIGHT
FUNDRAISING

17 Rules of the Road for Green Light Fundraising:

1. Sustainable fundraising is based on the nonprofit's stories of the lives that are transformed by its work;

2. The role of the development staff is to organize and communicate, organize and follow-up, and organize and be grateful;

3. Eighty percent of the funds raised each campaign cycle are raised by volunteers asking in person for a gift;

4. Twenty per cent of the funds are raised by letters, phone calls, and special events;

5. During the first year of sustainable fundraising, the lead gift is 15% of the goal;

6. The campaign chairperson is a widely known and respected community leader who lends credibility to the campaign;

7. Volunteers are energized to ask successfully the right five people for the right amount;

8. Volunteers ask people they know;

9. Staff of the nonprofit designs and manages smart and friendly systems that give volunteers the support they need to be successful;

10. Each volunteer chairperson serves for one campaign cycle and has a co-chairperson who will serve as chairperson for the next campaign cycle;

11. Volunteer leaders help recruit their team;

12. Team leaders recruit their own team of volunteer solicitors;

13. Team leaders track their volunteers' progress in asking for five gifts;

14. A weekly score card tracks the progress of each segment of the campaign;

15. Lead and major gifts are solicited during a quiet phase;

16. The public phase of the campaign is completed in four weeks from kickoff to wrap-up solicitation; and

17. Every success is celebrated.

 Need More Help From Rich? See p. 241

GREEN LIGHT
FUNDRAISING

Looking Ahead

When you learned how to drive, you memorized the rules of the road to pass your written driver's permit test. But when you passed the behind the wheel test, and then drove solo for the first time, you were nervous and excited. You hoped you'd remember the rules of the road but you weren't focused on the rules; you were focused on the roads ahead, your hands on the wheel, and other cars. You are about to get behind the wheel of Green Light Fundraising and it is exciting. In the next chapter, you're going to learn how to draw on the help of mentors, colleagues, and experts as you learn to "drive" a sustainable fundraising campaign from start to finish.

How can we improve?

E-mail us at (comment@greenlightfundraising.org) to let us know when something is unclear, or you have a suggestion for improving the book. Please identify the page and paragraph that needs improving.

GREEN LIGHT
FUNDRAISING

CHAPTER 3

The First Year Will Be The Hardest, or Truth in Advertising

"Fundraising books all make it sound so simple," a director of development said to me one day when I was consulting with her organization.

"When you combine 792 simple things what you have is complexity," I replied. The comment may not have been comforting but it was honest.

> Be not afraid of going slowly; be afraid only of standing still.
>
> ~Chinese Proverb

You and your organization are considering adapting a sustainable fundraising system because you are looking for a better way of fundraising. You've been struggling to raise the funds your organization needs to thrive as it carries out its mission of transforming your corner of the world.

Your organization has been holding off launching a fundraising program or upgrading your current program because of uncertainty.

Despite the uncertainty, you and your organization can no longer hold off. You need to raise funds even if you are uncertain how to go about it and whether you will succeed. Good. Thriving organizations embrace uncertainty as a way to discover new ways to produce their treasure. That's the wilderness path.

In chapter 1, I mentioned directing a capital campaign make it possible for a group of adults with developmental disabilities to move from a nursing home into a dozen small group homes. The campaign proved to be a trip into the wilderness for the CEO and me.

The wilderness path

Thriving organizations embrace uncertainty as a way to discover new ways to produce their treasure.

The CEO and the board of directors were committed to moving the residents out of the nursing home but the CEO did not want to do a capital campaign. The small group home project was going to create a lot of uncertainty in the organization and he didn't want to add to that uncertainty by having the organization undertake its first-ever capital campaign.

GREEN LIGHT
FUNDRAISING

Eventually, however, he and the board concluded that the project could only be done through the $1.2 million capital campaign. They embraced the uncertainty of a capital campaign as a way to "discover each person's hopes, dreams and desires, develop a network of supports, and provide opportunity for life experiences regardless of obstacles (http://www.horizonhouseperu.org/phil.htm.)"

The campaign was a wilderness journey for me because it was my first campaign and I didn't have a paid consultant to guide me. Thankfully the retired YMCA executive I mentioned earlier mentored me, but it was still a campaign filled with my mistakes and uncertainty.

Living in the nursing home limited the residents' ability to explore and discover their hopes, dreams, and desires. When the campaign was complete and the people were in their small homes, they had much more freedom. One young man promptly walked to a store a few blocks from his new home. Staff members were shocked. How did he know where the store was?

As you lead a sustainable fundraising campaign, you will discover that, like the young man who found his way to the store, you will find your way.

The Honor of Leading Sustainable Fundraising

Your organization is probably not considering sustainable fundraising because your CEO loves fundraising. Rather the CEO and board want to undertake sustainable fundraising because there is no other way to accomplish critical parts of your organization's mission except by a substantial increase in fundraising.

You've been tapped to head up this initiative because you are the director of development. You might consider taking the lead in developing sustainable fundraising as either exhilarating or terrifying. And it will be both of these.

But I suggest you also consider it an honor. You've been tapped to lead sustainable fundraising because it's critical to the mission of your organization. As you embrace the uncertainty of learning and implementing sustainable fundraising, you are transforming the lives of the people who are touched by your organization.

GREEN LIGHT
FUNDRAISING

Your organization may be an environmental organization. If so, through sustainable fundraising, you have the honor of playing a significant role in transforming the lives of people who are touched by the environment.

Your organization may be serving the seniors in your community. If so, through Green Light Fundraising, you have the honor of playing a significant role transforming the lives of older people who are trying to thrive amidst the uncertainty of the final stage of life.

Your organization may be a community arts or theater organization. If so, through sustainable fundraising, you have the honor of playing a significant role transforming the lives of artists, actors, playwrights, directors and producers as well as theater and arts lovers in your community.

Real leaders embrace uncertainty

As you study this book you'll find that each of the concepts, tools, and talents that fit together to form sustainable fundraising for your nonprofit are simple and readily understood. At the same time, as you begin to fit them into a plan for your nonprofit and begin to implement them you are likely to think, "What have I gotten myself into?"

Welcome to the wilderness path.

In all likelihood, you will experience a lot of uncertainty through the first complete cycle of sustainable fundraising. You and your executive director and board will begin recruiting the general chairperson for your first campaign and the first three people may turn you down. At that point you may well be wondering, "Is this sustainable fundraising going to work?"

You are not alone. You are simply a leader. Leaders often head into the unknown with the intent of learning their way to a new place. "We built the bridge as we walked on it," one business executive told Robert E. Quinn, a University of Michigan business professor, as he described how his company had undertaken a major change. (Quinn, Robert E. *Deep Change: Discovering the Leader Within.* Josey-Bass, San Francisco, 1996)

As nonprofit leaders, we need a better way of transferring the knowledge that nonprofits need to do successful fundraising. Evergreen Leaders does fundraising consulting. At the same time we are a nonprofit, constantly trying to discover new ways of giving information to our clients and to the whole nonprofit world to reduce consulting costs and increase the amount of funds raised that go directly to transforming the lives of the people each nonprofit serves.

This ebook is one way we are transferring knowledge to nonprofit organizations who meet the critical needs of people in our communities.

Real leaders find mentors

Use this ebook as a mentor and guide to establishing your organization's sustainable fundraising system. We'll also tell you enough stories along the way so that you'll know it's never as simple as it seems in fundraising books and stories that show you how rewarding using this system can be. You can set up a sustainable system that will help you raise significant funds the first year and will raise even more funds the second year.

And find your own Bill Glenn. Every region of the country has retired nonprofit leaders who have significant fundraising experience. Talk the sustainable fundraising tools, talents, and systems outlined in this book over with a mentor. The support of mentors will be invaluable in helping you make it through the wilderness of the first year of sustainable fundraising.

As mentioned in the Introduction you may want to consider joining the Green Light Fundraising Club. At $29 a month the Club is an affordable way for us to help you through the wilderness to your first successful sustainable fundraising campaign.

GREEN LIGHT
FUNDRAISING

Real leaders are rewarded

You will find that getting through the wilderness of the first cycle of sustainable fundraising is extremely rewarding:

1. You will be rewarded with the deep satisfaction of knowing you played a key role in raising funds that will transform the lives of people whom your organization serves.

2. You will be rewarded by knowing you played a key role in transforming your organization, because at the end of the first fundraising cycle, your organization will have the people, skills, and systems in place to grow in its ability to do sustainable fundraising.

3. You will be rewarded, whether you are a board member, CEO, or development director, with having learned systems and skills that will continue to help your organization and any other nonprofit you serve.

Looking Ahead

The first year of Green Light Fundraising will have its challenges but don't let that scare you.

Keep moving, even if slowly.

The next chapter gives you a detailed set of questions to help you assess the obstacles and opportunities to adapting sustainable fundraising in your organization. Information is king and when you work through the questions, you will have essential information to help you establish sustainable fundraising within your nonprofit.

How can we improve?

E-mail us at (comment@greenlightfundraising.org) to let us know when something is unclear, or you have a suggestion for improving the book. Please identify the page and paragraph that needs improving.

GREEN LIGHT
FUNDRAISING

CHAPTER 4

Discover The Paths And Obstacles To
Adopting Green Light Fundraising

"Suppose a king is about to go to war against another king," an ancient spiritual teacher said to a group of his disciples. "Will he not first sit down and consider whether he is able with ten thousand men to oppose the one coming against him with twenty thousand? If he is not able, he will send a delegation while the other is still a long way off and will ask for terms of peace."

Knowledge is power. Information is liberating. Education is the premise of progress, in every society, in every family.

— Kofi Annan, former U.N. Secretary General

You are probably not a king, and fundraising is definitely not a war, but Green Light Fundraising is a major undertaking, and you better discover if you have the resources you need to complete the first fundraising cycle.

Discovery is the time to be sweetly and brutally honest about your organization and the world around it.

Discovery is the time to be sweetly honest about the strengths of your organization, its mission, and its great success stories. Discovery is the time to brag about the people who make up your organization, your organization's place in the community, and all your organization's connections to community leaders and people with money. During discovery, you'll likely find you have more resources than you expected.

Discovery is also the time to be brutally honest about the shortcomings of your organization. Your organization may have a board with members who hate fundraising. It wouldn't be the first board that is made up of people who would rather have a root canal than ask someone for money. Your organization may have had a scandal that hit the papers three years ago. After being brutally honest in the discovery phase, your organization may need to fix a couple of things before launching your first sustainable campaign.

Sustainable fundraising begins with discovery because all the wonderful and difficult things you discover become building blocks when you reach the next phase—designing your map to sustainable fundraising.

GREEN LIGHT
FUNDRAISING

The following questions have plenty of room to take good notes during the discovery phase. Some of the questions you can answer yourself. Other questions, you will have to discuss with other staff or board members to answer. Still others will require research. Some questions can be skipped because they don't apply to your organization or community.

Some of the discovery questions below may reveal an iceberg. When you one of the discovery questions reveals the tip of the iceberg, ask follow-up questions to get a good picture of the entire iceberg.

For instance, when I am consulting and ask a question about the client's board's ability to raise funds, I may be told, "Our board is not a fundraising board." I follow up with detailed questions to determine how many of the board members give and whether any of the board members have been involved with fundraising programs for other nonprofits. I might ask if any of the board members have close friends in the community who have raised funds for other nonprofits or community projects. You get the idea. Discover. Discover. Discover.

Take detailed notes because when you get to the design and implementation phases, your notes will contain lots of nuggets of information that you will use in those phases.

By the way, if you are the kind of person who wants to see the broad picture before diving into the details, check out The Quick Guide to the Design Phase in chapter 6. The Quick Guide sketches the key components of the campaign. All the questions in the discovery phase are linked to one or more of the components in the design and implementation phases.

Have fun in your discovery. If you've read this far in this ebook, you are highly motivated to learn sustainable fundraising. As you work through the following questions, you'll discover the raw materials to develop a healthy, sustainable fundraising system for your organization.

At Evergreen Leaders we've developed the 7 Paths of Thriving Organizations, a framework used by EGL consultants to teach nonprofit leaders and supervisors how to help their organizations thrive.

Fundraising is a leadership role and the 7 Paths work equally well as a framework to create a sustainable fundraising program tailored to your organization.

GREEN LIGHT
FUNDRAISING

Discovery

Treasure Path

Each nonprofit offers the world a treasure by transforming the lives of a specific group of people who struggle with a specific need.

Fundraising is an emotional business and a relationship business. People give when they are moved and they give when they are asked by someone they respect. Here are a series of questions that help us discover your organization's treasure path:

1. What is the mission of your organization in one short, memorable sentence?

2. When is your organization at its best?

3. What are the stories of struggle and transformation of the people served by your organization?

4. How are the stories currently being told?

5. How are donors given the opportunity to experience the struggle and transformation of the lives of the people your nonprofit serves?

6. How are donors bonding to the nonprofit?

Talent Path

Organizations thrive by harnessing the strengths and working around the weaknesses of individuals. Some people are weak in one area of talents needed to do sustainable fundraising and strong in other areas. Successful sustainable fundraising depends on fitting together all the talents needed.

We use the following questions to discover the talents your organization can tap into to do sustainable fundraising:

GREEN LIGHT
FUNDRAISING

1. What talents does your executive director have that can benefit your fundraising efforts? What weaknesses of the executive director related to fundraising will you have to work around in the design stage?

2. What talents does your development director have that can benefit your fundraising efforts? What weaknesses of the development director related to fundraising will you have to work around in the design stage?

3. Who from the nonprofit is nurturing a relationship with your top donors? How?

4. Who are the people who have an ongoing relationship with the nonprofit who are being asked to give? Board? Staff? Volunteers? People served? Families of those served? Vendors? Neighbors? Others?

5. Who are the people not be asked?

6. Who, among the people your organization serves, would be a good representative of your organization to the press, potential donors, and volunteer fundraisers?

7. Who currently connected with your organization has a talent for asking people face to face for money?

8. Who, among the people your organization serves as well as those being served, has a gift for telling stories of struggle and transformation? Verbally? In writing?

9. Who in your organization is most connected with major donors or potential donors?

10. Who are the top five people in your community who have the respect and ability to serve as general chairperson of your campaign?

11. Who in your organization has connections with each of the five general chairperson candidates and will be helpful in recruiting the general chairperson?

12. Who in your community has a talent for recruiting people to ask for money?

13. Who in your organization has a talent for writing? Who has the ability to write powerful fundraising letters based on a story from someone who has benefited from your organization's services?

14. Who loves to keep the many practical details (volunteer packets, media packets, donor and prospect lists, etc.) organized?

15. Who loves to keep the systems running smoothly?

GREEN LIGHT
FUNDRAISING

Need More Help From Rich? See p. 241

Ecosystem Path

Organizations thrive on a healthy, improvisational relationship with their environment. To raise funds effectively, each nonprofit must understand the ecosystem in which it operates and the opportunities for fundraising that the ecosystem offers. As part of discovering the ecosystem, and the opportunities it offers for sustainable fundraising, answer the following questions:

1. Who are the top ten volunteers who lead fundraising campaigns in your community and what is your organization's connection to them?

2. Who are the top ten philanthropists in your community and what is your organization's connection to them?

3. Who are the leading fundraising nonprofits in your community? What approaches do they use?

4. What organizations in your community currently raise money for services similar to yours? What distinguishes your organization from them?

5. Describe your Board's connections that can benefit your organization's fundraising efforts.

6. Has your organization been the subject of negative press or negative rumors in the last five years? If so, how did your organization handle it?

7. How engaged are your organization's staff members in representing your organization positively to friends and neighbors?

8. How does your organization stay in touch with people served in the past (alumni)?

9. How does your organization stay in touch with families of those served?

10. How does your organization stay in touch with current donors?

11. What local foundations serve your community and what is your organization's relationship with them?

12. What is your organization's relationship to political leaders who are part of your organization's ecosystem?

13. What is your organization's relationship with celebrities or other well-known people in your community?

GREEN LIGHT
FUNDRAISING

14. What is your organization's relationship with community leaders who influence the success of fundraising efforts in your community?

15. To what businesses and community organizations is your organization connected?

16. If your organization receives funds from United Way, does United Way restrict your fundraising during their campaign season? If so, when is their campaign season?

17. What is the local business climate?

18. How does the community view your organization and its leadership?

Smart and Friendly Systems

Organizations thrive or shrivel based on the systems they set up to produce the treasure, i.e. to transform the lives of those they serve. Likewise, systems support or hinder effective sustainable fundraising.

Here is a set of questions to discover the fundraising systems currently in place in your organization:

1. How well does the organization's current fundraising database support the organization's fundraising?

2. Does the organization accept online donations?

3. Does your board have a fundraising committee? If so, who is on the committee?

4. What systems does your organization currently use for raising major gifts? Mid-size gifts? Small gifts?

5. Rank the systems by effectiveness.

6. Who are the top ten donors and who relates to them?

7. Who are the top one hundred donors and who relates to them?

8. What are the current systems for identifying potential donors?

9. What are the systems for thank you letters, phone calls, and visits?

10. What systems does the organization use to communicate with donors? Potential donors?

11. What systems does the organization have in place to connect with media used by donors and potential donors?

Need More Help From Rich? See p. 241

GREEN LIGHT FUNDRAISING

Humble hierarchy path

Humble hierarchy leaders have little personal ambition, an unwavering will to help the organization transform the lives of those it serves, and a passion to create space for all to thrive. Leaders with this passion will draw many into the process of fundraising, equipping them to have an impact in reaching the organization's fundraising goals. To assess the attitudes of leadership to the process of sustainable fundraising, we ask the following questions:

1. How committed to sustainable fundraising is your organization's board?
2. How committed to sustainable fundraising is top leadership?
3. How committed to sustainable fundraising are key staff leaders?
4. How committed to sustainable fundraising are other key leaders?
5. If commitment is lagging, how can it be increased?
6. What part of sustainable fundraising is the executive director willing to delegate and which part do they see as part of his or her role?

Wilderness Path

Thriving organizations embrace uncertainty as a way to discover new ways to produce their treasure. Sustainable fundraising is a journey into uncertainty to seek a new and better way to fund the transforming of lives that your organization does. To help your organization prepare for the journey into the unknown to develop sustainable fundraising, we ask the following questions:

1. How ready are board, staff and key volunteers to embrace the uncertainty inherent in creating a sustainable system of fundraising? What can be done to help them prepare to embrace the uncertainty?
2. Does the organization have a good, experienced coach, mentor, or consultant for making the transition to sustainable fundraising?

GREEN LIGHT
FUNDRAISING

Rhythm Path

Thriving organizations honor the work and life rhythms of their people. Also, organizations and communities have rhythms that make some times of the year better than others to launch the asking phases of sustainable fundraising campaigns. Here are questions designed to help us discover the work and life rhythms of your organization and community that will shape the design of your sustainable fundraising.

1. Does your organization have funding cycles that impact when to do the asking phase of the campaign? If so, how?

2. Will vacations of key staff affect when the asking phase of the campaign is scheduled?

3. Are there key prospective campaign leaders or volunteers who are snowbirds? If so, when do they leave and when do they return?

4. What other regular fundraising activities taking place in your community will affect when you schedule the asking phases of your campaign?

To make it easier for you answer the questions, you can find a Word document with the discovery questions at http://greenlightfundraising.org/downloads/discovery.doc

Looking Ahead

When you work through the questions in this chapter, you gather a lot of data that will be   helpful in designing your sustainable fundraising campaign. Now you are ready to begin preparations for the campaign. In the next chapter you'll learn the essential tools such as creating a gift chart to use in testing a tentative goal. You'll also learn the questions to ask the board and key constituents to assess the feasibility of reaching the potential goal.

How can we improve?

E-mail us at (comment@greenlightfundraising.org) to let us know when something is unclear, or you have a suggestion for improving the book. Please identify the page and paragraph that needs improving.

GREEN LIGHT
FUNDRAISING

CHAPTER 5

Prepare, Prepare Before You Ask

I learned about the importance of preparation the hard way. When I first began fundraising consulting, my church conference and mission board contracted with me to help them with a three year, $600,000 campaign. The missions committee was enthused and pressed me to help them get the campaign under way. They needed to start asking as soon as possible because nine local and global mission projects were depending on them. They were sure the money was there; we just needed people to ask for the gifts.

> "It doesn't hurt to ask"
>
> Actually, it does hurt. It does hurt to ask the wrong way, to ask without preparation, to ask without permission. It hurts because you never get another chance to ask right.
>
> — Posted by Seth Godin on Seth's Blog on May 18, 2009

I surrendered to their urgency and confidence and began to plan and move ahead without doing a feasibility study. Since then I've discovered that almost all our clients have an urgent need for funds and want to move ahead with asking for gifts as quickly as possible.

At the end of three years, the missions campaign raised $279,623, well short of the $600,000 goal. Like marketing guru Seth Godin, I learned that sometimes it does hurt to ask because you can fall short of your goal if you have not done a good job of preparation.

Every organization has stakeholders. Before launching a new initiative like Green Light or sustainable fundraising, an organization needs to determine the commitment to the initiative of each group of stakeholders such as board, staff, donors, volunteers, suppliers, and community leaders. While sustainable fundraising, like most organizational change, does not usually start with universal acclaim, it's helpful to know who strongly supports the initiative and whose support needs to be carefully cultivated.

In chapter four we provided you with an extensive set of discovery questions, the questions that you need to be able to answer in order to direct a successful campaign.

In this chapter we identify a much smaller set of questions that the organization's key leaders need to be able to answer as part of their testing whether to proceed with green light fundraising.

GREEN LIGHT
FUNDRAISING

Depending on the type of governance your organization has, your board of directors may expect to approve a new initiative such as sustainable fundraising. If they need to approve the sustainable fundraising campaign, the executive director and development director will jointly need to develop the proposal. An executive director should have a sense as to how detailed the proposal should be. You may want to include the 17 rules of the road for sustainable fundraising from chapter two. You may also want to include a timeline like the one we cover in chapter six.

It's not necessary to hire a consultant to do a formal feasibility study prior to launching sustainable fundraising but as part of the proposal to the board. Certainly prior to launching sustainable fundraising, the CEO and board of the organization need to set a tentative goal and develop a gift chart as part of testing that goal with the board and key constituents.

In all likelihood we have an Italian economist, Vilfredo Pareto, to thank for the gift chart. In the early 20th century he studied economic distributions in Italy. He discovered that 80% of the land was owned by 20% of the people. He noted a similar distribution of wealth.

At some point, fundraisers discovered that contributions to a campaign follow a similar pattern, with 80% of the total amount raised coming from 20% of the donors. Gift charts usually start with a lead gift of 10% of the total goal and show the number of gifts needed at each level to meet the goal distributing the gifts across the chart so that 80% of the income comes from 20% of the donors.

When I work with clients to create their sustainable fundraising plan for the first time, I usually encourage them to set the lead gift at 15% of the total goal. For instance, if their goal is to raise $200,000 the first year, I encourage them to set a goal for the lead gift of $30,000 (15% x $200,000 = $30,000). They can keep the lead gift at $30,000 for several years while the total income raised each year grows to as much as $300,000. When the lead gift becomes less that 10% of the annual goal, it's time to increase the level of the lead gift.

Establishing the goal for your first sustainable fundraising campaign is a combination of the organization's need and an assessment of how much the constituency can be expected to give. I encourage organizations to be conservative in setting their first year's goal because it's important to succeed the first year in order to create momentum for succeeding years.

GREEN LIGHT
FUNDRAISING

Let's assume that the executive director and the development director have discussed the organization's need for funds and have made an educated guess that the constituency of the organization will be able to give $100,000 the first year. Once the staff leadership has set a tentative goal, the next step is assessing the constituency's ability to give in order to confirm or revise the goal.

Creating a gift chart for the tentative goal is a good tool to use in assessing the goal. Blackbaud has a gift range calculator on their website at http://www.blackbaud.com/company/resources/giftrange/giftcalc.aspx. You can also use the Gift Range Calculator tool at http://www.giftrangecalculator.com/

Blackbaud assumes a 10% of goal lead gift while Gift Range Calculator assumes a 25% of goal lead gift but, as I've already mentioned, I suggest setting 15% of the campaign goal for the lead gift. Still, using the Blackbaud gift calculator will be a good guide for developing your own gift chart. Remember the 80-20 rule. Expect eighty percent of your goal to come from twenty percent of your donors.

Here's a sample gift chart:

Gift Chart for $100,000

Segment	# of gifts	Size of gift	Total
Lead	1	$15,000.00	$15,000.00
Advance	1	$10,000.00	$10,000.00
Advance	2	$7,500.00	$15,000.00
Advance	3	$5,000.00	$15,000.00
Advance	4	$2,500.00	$10,000.00
Advance	6	$1,500.00	$9,000.00
Special	9	$1,000.00	$9,000.00
Special	12	$500.00	$6,000.00
Special	20	$250.00	$5,000.00
Special	30	$100.00	$3,000.00
Under $100	Varies	$3,000.00	$3,000.00
		TOTAL:	$100,000.00

GREEN LIGHT
FUNDRAISING

Once you have the gift chart, I suggest describing the reason for the campaign to the organization's board and key members of the constituency. Then show them the gift chart to let them know the range of gifts needed for the campaign to succeed, and then ask the following questions:

1. Does the organization have good connections with 3-4 people who have the ability to give the lead gift?

2. Is the organization likely to be able to raise the other upper level gifts needed for the campaign to be successful?

3. Does the community see the nonprofit as meeting a genuine need?

4. Does the community see the organization as pursuing its mission in an effective and fiscally-responsible manner?

5. Does the community have confidence in the nonprofit and its leaders?

6. If the campaign focuses on a specific project, will the community see the project as worthwhile?

The response you get from the above abbreviated feasibility study will help you either confirm the goal or revise it.

As the executive director and development director prepare the proposal for the board, they should identify and talk to a potential champion on the board—the person on the board who is most likely to grasp the value of Green Light Fundraising and be willing to champion it to the whole board.

The champion may be the board president or a member with experience in serving as a fundraising volunteer. Go over the sustainable fundraising proposal with the likely champion and make sure you've answered all their questions.

As the missions campaign that I mentioned earlier in this chapter progressed, it became apparent that key stakeholders were not as committed to the campaign as we needed to be successful. Since we had not identified the reservations of key stakeholders, we were not able to build support with them prior to starting to ask.

GREEN LIGHT
FUNDRAISING

There are three other areas of preparation for a successful campaign that take time:

- Identifying and communicating the stories of how the organization transforms lives;

- Recruiting the right campaign leaders and volunteer solicitors;

- And creating smart and friendly support systems to make it possible for volunteers to ask confidently and successfully for five gifts.

It takes preparation to design a sustainable fundraising campaign that delights volunteers, moves donors to give generously, and surpasses its goal. As rule number two of the rules of the road for Green Light Fundraising states: The role of the development staff is to organize and communicate, organize and follow-up, and organize and be grateful.

Looking ahead

Now you are ready for chapter six where you will learn how to design your sustainable fundraising campaign so that all the pieces fit together in a time sequence that works.

How can we improve?

E-mail us at (comment@greenlightfundraising.org) to let us know when something is unclear, or you have a suggestion for improving the book. Please identify the page and paragraph that needs improving.

GREEN LIGHT
FUNDRAISING

CHAPTER 6

Your Quick Guide To The Design Phase

Since the early 1980s, various management writers have recounted versions of the following story first told in a poem, "Brief Thoughts on Maps" by Miroslav Holub, first published in 1977 in the *Times Literary Supplement.*

One winter a young Hungarian lieutenant sent a small group of soldiers on a reconnaissance mission into the Alps. Much to his dismay it snowed for two days straight and the soldiers did not return.

On the third day, the detachment of soldiers returned. "How did you find your way back?" asked the lieutenant. The soldiers reported that they had given up hope when one of them found a map in his pocket. Encouraged, they set up camp and waited out the storm. When the snow stopped, they used the map to get their bearings and they made it out.

When the lieutenant asked to see the "remarkable map" he discovered that it was "not a map of the Alps but of the Pyrenees."

It seems wild but the wrong map may be better than no map. I promise you that your first timeline for your campaign will not be perfect but it will be a lot better than no map.

Mapping the commitment to sustainable fundraising

Often, when I begin to work with a client, they want to launch their sustainable fundraising campaign within a few months. I don't tell them no but I give them a caution light rather than a green light.

In the first campaign that I directed, my executive director and I planned to be raising money in a few months. A few months went by and we still didn't have the campaign chairperson. Not that we hadn't tried. The fifth person we asked agreed to be the chairperson (see Chapter 10 for details on recruiting the campaign chairperson). There was no way that we could recruit all the volunteer leaders and solicitors to do the solicitation in the time that we first projected. We put off the solicitation phase for a year and that gave us time to have all our ducks in a row. The campaign was successful but it never would have succeeded if we had stuck with our original timeline.

Need More Help From Rich? See p. 241

GREEN LIGHT
FUNDRAISING

Before you begin designing the actual campaign, you and your executive director need to create a timeline for each of the phases it will take to adapt sustainable fundraising. There will be variations with every organization. It may be a board member is the initial advocate of the adoption of sustainable fundraising. Here's a table that can assist you in mapping the time it will take for your organization to commit fully to the campaign:

Month	Action
	Executive director and development director commit to sustainable fundraising
	Determine whether organization will use consultant.
	Create proposal for board approval
	Select consultant

Once the key people in your organization are committed to the campaign, you are ready to map the campaign.

Designing the campaign phases

Before you can begin recruiting the volunteers to help your campaign succeed, you need a map, a timeline that shows the volunteers exactly when they are needed for each phase. The timeline also helps the executive director and development staff to plan the campaign to fit the natural rhythms of the organization and your community. For instance, some local United Ways restrict member organizations from raising funds during certain time periods. In that case, your timeline will help you to plan around the United Way blackout period. The timeline helps the development director to manage the campaign so that staff can provide excellent support to volunteers at every stage of the campaign.

Managing a campaign is a complex task. It's like juggling. If you have too many balls in the air at one time, you are sure to drop one or more. A timeline can help you make sure that you aren't scheduling two kickoffs at the same time or scheduling two back-to-to meetings 20 miles apart. A timeline can help you to juggle three balls at a time instead of fifteen.

You may feel like there are a lot of variables that you don't know that will affect your timeline. Still it's a good discipline to create a time line for the campaign, knowing that you can fine tune it later.

GREEN LIGHT
FUNDRAISING

At this stage of reading this book you may look at the timeline below and see that it references items that I have not covered yet. That's okay. I included the timeline in this chapter because it's an essential tool to use early in the campaign. One you have completed the book, you can come back to this chapter and you'll be ready to start with the first draft of your own timeline.

One of my friends, who has lead several sustainable fundraising campaigns, says she gets by with less meetings than are listed in the example below. For instance, she meets individually with chairpersons and also does a lot with reporting by e-mail, rather than having report meetings. I'm including the complete timeline below even though you may be able to alter it fit your community. Also, you may need fewer meetings in subsequent years once you and your volunteer leaders have learned the Green Light Fundraising system.

Here's an example of a timeline:

Date	Timeline/ date	Action/Event	Who
January year one		First Pre-campaign Committee meeting	
Jan		Begin work on case statement	Director of Dev.
March		Complete recruiting general chairperson	Pre-Campaign Comm.
March		Complete final draft of case statement	Director of Dev.
April		Start monthly campaign committee meeting to oversee recruiting & marketing & lead gift solicitation	Campaign chairperson
April		Recruit marketing comm.	Dir. Of Dev., Ex. Dir., Campaign Chairperson
April		Establish speakers bureau	
April		Design e-letter that will encourage volunteers and report on progress	Dir. Of Dev.

May		Test case statement & e-letter with marketing comm. Revise and submit to graphic designer (if you are using one)	Dir. Of Dev. & Marketing Comm.
May		Recruit Advance Gifts Chairperson	Campaign Comm.
June		Test design of case statement	Ex. Dir. Dev. Dir. Marketing Comm.
June		Recruit Special Gifts Chairperson	Campaign Comm.
July		Print the case statement	Dir. of Dev.
July-August	Summer break	July-August	Summer break for campaign committee
September		Complete recruiting of members of Advance gifts team	Advance Gifts Chairperson
September		Complete solicitation of lead gift	Pre-Campaign Comm. Campaign chair, board chair, Ex. Dir
September		Complete recruiting of Special Gifts team members	Chairperson
September		Recruit Board and Staff Inner Circle Chairpersons	Board chair, Ex Dir., Dev. Dir.
September		Complete recruiting staff Inner Circle staff team	Staff Inner Circle Chairperson
September		Board and staff inner circle kickoffs	Inner Circle chairpersons
October	First week of	Celebrate success of inner circle	Dev. Dir. & Chairpersons
		Kickoff advance gifts phase of campaign	

GREEN LIGHT
FUNDRAISING

September		Complete recruiting of five special gifts team leaders	Special Gifts chairperson
October		Complete inner circle	Inner circle chairperson
October		Complete recruiting of special gifts team members	Special gifts team leaders
November		Celebrate successful completion of the advance gifts phase	Adv. Gifts chair, Campaign chair, Ex. Dir. , Dev. Dir.
January second year		Special gifts kickoff	
January		Media blitz	Dev. Dir., Mktg. Comm.
February	End of second week of Feb.	Campaign wrap-up and celebration	

The director of development is responsible for creating the timeline and managing any change to the timeline. After you have created your first draft of the campaign timeline, test it out with your executive director. He or she may spot some areas where it needs immediate adjustment.

The above timeline gives the broad strokes of the campaign. You will also need to create further timelines for marketing and the advance gifts and special gifts phases. The marketing timeline will have precise dates for each date that you will accomplish each item in your marketing campaign. Each solicitation phase will have a weekly report meeting for team leaders. We'll cover those in later chapters.

You can find a template of this table as a Word document on the Green Light Fundraising website at http://greenlightfundraising.org/downloads/timeline.doc.

Mapping money

There's an old adage, "It takes money to make money." Your executive director and board are going to want to know how much money it will take to meet your sustainable fundraising goal. Below is a sample budget from an organization that was going to move to a sustainable fundraising model and increase their giving by $200,000 in the first year.

Need More Help From Rich? See p. 241 GREEN LIGHT FUNDRAISING

You'll notice that I didn't include the salary of the development director but did include the salary of an additional part time assistant to make the sustainable fundraising campaign possible. You'll also notice that the campaign covered two fiscal years and thus the budget is divided up by fiscal years. You can use the budget below as a template for developing your own campaign budget. You can find an Excel spread sheet with the budget template on the Evergreen Leaders website at http://greenlightfundraising.org/downloads/budget.xls.

Sustainable Fundraising Budget			
	FY2010	FY2011	TOTAL
Support Staff	$7,650.00	$15,600.00	$23,250.00
FICA. Medicare, Workers Comp, Unemployment	$1,530.00	$3,120.00	$4,650.00
Consulting Fees	$8,280.00	$6,440.00	$14,720.00
Printing & Marketing			
Case statement (500)	$1,118.00		$1,118.00
Brochure (1000)	$250.00		$250.00
Pledge Cards (1000)	$100.00		$100.00
Campaign e-letter	$180.00	$90.00	$270.00
Meetings			
Meals & Snacks	$300.00	$500.00	$800.00
Postage	$100.00	$500.00	$600.00
Office Supplies	$200.00	$200.00	$400.00
TOTAL	$19,708.00	$26,450.00	$46,158.00

In praise of being well-organized

When I did my first campaign as a development director, our Special Gifts Chairperson, a retired aeronautics executive, kept telling me, "This campaign is over organized." At the time I wondered if his criticism was warranted. No more. A campaign is a complex undertaking involving staff and dozens of volunteers. The role of the development director is to organize the campaign in such a way that everyone is clear about their roles and the expectations you have for them. You organize the campaign to make it as easy as possible for every volunteer to succeed.

GREEN LIGHT
FUNDRAISING

After my first kickoff meeting with a group of volunteer solicitors, I was reporting to my mentor how it went and he asked, "Did you have an agenda?"

"No."

"You always want an agenda at a meeting because then you can relax in the meeting."

After that conversation I never went into a meeting without an agenda. Not only could I relax, because I knew all the key issues would be addressed, but it helped the volunteers relax as well. The volunteer chairperson of the meeting knew exactly what items needed to be covered and so did the participants. Everyone could relax and be productive.

You want to recruit volunteer leaders who are used to getting things done and getting things done promptly. Most will appreciate having the campaign well-organized.

Looking ahead

Why should I care?

That's the first question you need to answer for your potential sustainable fundraising volunteers and donors.

You provide the answer to "Why should I care?" in a case statement. In the next two chapters you will learn how to write a powerful case statement that can be used throughout the campaign to help people care deeply about your cause. Volunteers who care will give freely of their time and donors who care will give generously of their money to help you transform lives. These next two chapters are exciting.

How can we improve?

E-mail us at (comment@greenlightfundraising.org) to let us know when something is unclear, or you have a suggestion for improving the book. Please identify the page and paragraph that needs improving.

GREEN LIGHT FUNDRAISING

CHAPTER 7

Making The Case 101: Stories of Transformed Lives

Nonprofits Always Need to Raise Funds For a Cold Day in January

By Dave McClure. Executive Director, Youth Service Bureau

One morning last January, before I could get my coat off and on the hook, a young social worker on staff asked me, "Where can I find someone to work on a camper furnace?"

"Why do you ask?"

"Well, I have this family" she began "and they're living in a campground in this trailer. Pretty big trailer really but the furnace went out."

"What are they doing for heat?" I asked. It was, after all, 16 degrees below zero.

"Space heaters" she said "they've been hauling water for a while. Remember? This is the family I was going to take a turkey to at Christmas but they said they would burn up too much propane cooking it so I cooked it here at the office and took it to them."

"The husband is on disability," she continued. "The mom was off work due to an injury but is now laid off. The youngest is autistic and receives SSI. So they're making it on his disability and SSI. Four kids, three dogs. The smallest dog bit me when I took the turkey over."

"Call Stan ---"I said. Stan is the plumbing and sheet metal guy who installed the furnace at YSB. "He probably doesn't do campers but he'll know who does. Wait, I have his number."

An hour later I heard back from my worker. "Stan called me back" she said "and he knows a guy. I have a call in to him."

"Great."

"What about payment?" she said.

"Tell the guy we'll pay" I said "we'll sort it out after the heat's back on. That's why we're raising funds."

 Need More Help From Rich? See p. 241

GREEN LIGHT
FUNDRAISING

Nonprofits and fundraising are built on stories—stories of what is and stories of what could be. In this chapter we focus on how to write great stories to be used in your case statement for your campaign.

Every nonprofit starts when someone sees the way things are and imagines how they might be better. Our rural county has a medical clinic for the uninsured started by a nurse who had a major medical issue while she was between jobs. Suddenly she discovered first-hand what it is like to be without insurance.

She realized that she wasn't the only person without insurance in our county. She imagined a clinic designed to serve the uninsured. When she recovered from her illness, she founded a nonprofit, the Bureau County Health and Wellness Center. Local doctors volunteer at the clinic and someone without insurance can see a doctor for $10.

Stories of lives transformed by the work of a nonprofit organization help potential donors understand both the work of the organization and the need for their gift.

This ebook is the work of Evergreen Leaders, a nonprofit that helps nonprofits thrive through leadership and fundraising consulting and teaching. When we began to write the case statement for the sustainable campaign that made this ebook possible, we searched for stories that portrayed the treasure of transformed lives through sustainable fundraising.

Every nonprofit has stories about its efforts to transform lives. The challenge is to dip into the endless flow of stories to net core stories that will help potential donors to make a powerful connection to the lives transformed by the work of the nonprofit and to move them to help transform lives through a gift.

The first story we tried out in the case statement fell flat. It was a dramatic story from a client but it did not vividly portray the connection between sustainable fundraising and the work of transforming lives. Then we came across the story in the sidebar written by Dave McClure, the executive director of Youth Service Bureau of Illinois Valley, a former client whom we mentioned in the introduction of this book. In their first year of sustainable fundraising, YSB increased their fundraising by nearly 800%.

GREEN LIGHT
FUNDRAISING

Finding the story

How do you recognize a powerful core story that you can use effectively to portray the way your nonprofit transforms lives?

A few years ago two brothers, Chip Heath and Dan Heath, asked themselves, "Why do some ideas survive and others die?" Urban legends, conspiracy theories, and bogus public-health scares seem to fly from person to person. Yet, they noted, "people with important ideas—businessmen, educators, politicians, journalists, and others—struggle to make their ideas "stick."

Let's add fundraisers and nonprofit leaders to their list of people with important ideas.

Through extensive research the Heath brothers identified and wrote about six principles of sticky ideas in *Made to Stick: Why Some Ideas Die and Others Survive.*

Let's look at Dave McClure's story and see how it matches up with the six principles.

Principle 1: Simplicity

First, strip down the idea to its core. Be masters of exclusion. Relentlessly prioritize. Being short is not the mission, they caution:

> *... sound bites are not the ideal. Proverbs are the ideal. We must create ideas that are both simple and profound. The Golden Rule is the ultimate model of simplicity: a one-sentence statement so profound that an individual could spend a lifetime learning to follow it.*

When Dave McClure wrote the story to supporters, he was portraying the work of his nonprofit, an organization that helps youth and families succeed, and he was emphasizing the value of the gifts that people give to his organization.

Our purpose in selecting the story for our case statement was to portray how our sustainable fundraising system helps transform lives. But that's not a sticky idea. Very few people would read the opening sentence of this paragraph and find it memorable and easy to repeat. Words like transform, system, and sustainable are the opposite of simplicity. They are full of abstraction.

Need More Help From Rich? See p. 241

GREEN LIGHT
FUNDRAISING

To make it sticky we stripped it down to its core in our headline. The headline echoes like a proverb.

Nonprofits always need to raise funds for a cold day in January.

Principle 2: Unexpectedness

"How do we get our audience to pay attention to our ideas, and how do we maintain their interest when we need time to get the ideas across?" the Heath brothers asked.

First, surprise people. "We can use surprise — an emotion whose function is to increase alertness and cause focus — to grab people's attention."

Second, since surprise works only in the short term, they add that people who want to make their ideas stick need "to engage people's curiosity over a long period of time by systematically 'opening gaps' in their knowledge — and then filling those gaps."

We use the unexpected in our headline to Dave's story. It starts out with a generality, "Nonprofits always need to raise funds..." and then switches to the highly concrete... "for a cold day in January." The headline is designed to create curiosity and pull the reader into the story.

A story, by its nature, systematically creates "opening gaps" in the knowledge of the reader or listener and then fills in those gaps. When I wrote a novel, I didn't have a detailed outline. I approached each day's writing much as reader would: What's going to happen next?

Dave's story starts out with a question from a young social worker on staff: "Where can I find someone to work on a camper furnace?" Readers immediately wonder, as Dave did, why there was the need to work on a camper furnace. The story keeps creating gaps in our knowledge right to the end when the social worker asks, "What about payment?"

Dave fills in that gap in her knowledge and the knowledge of the reader when he says, "Tell the guy we'll pay" I said "we'll sort it out after the heat's back on. That's why we're raising funds."

GREEN LIGHT
FUNDRAISING

Principle 3: Concreteness

"How do we make our ideas clear?" the Heath brothers asked. Unfortunately, this is where nonprofit and business communications often fall short. As the *Made to Stick* authors note, "Mission statements, synergies, strategies, visions — they are often ambiguous to the point of being meaningless."

I once helped a nonprofit I was part of develop a mission statement. It sounded good when we completed it. A few months later we had some outside consultants reviewing the life and work of the nonprofit. When we mentioned that we had developed a one-sentence mission statement, one of the consultants asked to see it. One of our leaders handed him a folder. He read the mission statement and then looked up at us. "Can you tell me your mission statement?" he asked. None of us could. It was full of abstractions and we could not remember it, even though it was one sentence long.

Concrete means sensory. "Naturally sticky ideas are full of concrete images— ice-filled bathtubs, apples with razors — because our brains are wired to remember concrete data," the Heath brothers say.

A cold day in January is sensory. So is a proverb like "A bird in hand is worth two in the bush." You can feel the bird, you can see the bird, and you can see the bush. The proverb is a powerful way of communicating an abstract concept: it's better to go with what you have than to keep waiting for something better.

Principle 4: Credibility

"How do we make people believe our ideas?" asked the Heath brothers.

Most of us are not acknowledged authorities in a field and, thus, when we speak, people don't accept our ideas without skepticism. Telling a story about your cause with concrete details adds to the credibility.

Dave McClure's story has concrete details that add to its credibility. In describing the family the social worker says, "Four kids, three dogs. The smallest dog bit me when I took the [Christmas] turkey over."

GREEN LIGHT
FUNDRAISING

You believe in Dave's organization when you read that a small dog bit the social worker who was bringing a Christmas turkey and now that same social worker is trying to find a way to repair their furnace.

Principle 5: Emotions

How do we get people to care about our ideas? asked the Heath brothers.

Mother Teresa made an observation that answers the question when she said, "If I look at the mass, I will never act. If I look at the one, I will."

"Research done at Carnegie Mellon University and the University of Pennsylvania, and later summarized in *Made to Stick*, backs up Mother Teresa's observation. Researchers offered participants $5 to complete a survey on technology (irrelevant to the study). When the participants finished the survey they were given five $1 bills. Unexpectedly, they were also given an envelope with one of two versions of an appeal letter for an international aid organization, Save the Children.

Participants were left alone after being told they could read the letter and, if they wanted to, make a gift by putting it in the envelope, sealing it, and handing it to the researcher.

One version asked for a gift based on statistics from several countries such as "Food shortages in Malawi are affecting more than three million children" and "More than 11 million people in Ethiopia need immediate food assistance."

The second version told the story of seven-year old Rokia from Mali who "faces the severe threat of hunger or even starvation. Her life will be changed for the better as the result of your financial donation."

In response to the statistics-based appeal, participants donated $1.14 on average while, in response to the Rokia letter, participants donated over twice as much--$2.38.

The researchers pondered the results and decided that the emotion of the Rokia letter increased giving while the analytical thinking spurred by the statistics decreased giving. To test this theory, the researchers did a second study. This time they primed one group of participants to be emotional by asking them to write down one word

they think of when they hear the word "baby."

The second group they primed to think analytically by asking them to solve a problem: "If an object travels five feet per minute, then by your calculations, how many feet would it travel in 360 seconds?"

Then both groups were given the Rokia letter. The group that had just been thinking analytically gave $1.26 while the group who had been primed to be emotional gave $2.34.

"The results were shocking," said the Heath brothers. "The mere act of calculation reduced people's charity. Once we put on our analytical hat, we react to emotional appeals differently. We hinder our ability to feel."

Dave McClure's story focuses on one family living in a camper in January with a broken furnace. The story helps us care because one family is in danger.

Principle 6: Stories

"How do we get people to act on our ideas?" asked the Heath brothers.

Tell stories.

"In your presentations and informal meetings, telling and exchanging stories are at the core of rapport, relationship building, and creating a buying atmosphere," says sales guru and author Jeffrey Gitomer.

Stories create a giving atmosphere. When I began to work with Dave McClure's organization, helping them to establish sustainable fundraising, I quickly saw that Dave, who had been an executive director for over 25 years, was well-schooled in presenting his organization. He could easily describe the programs and statistics associated his organization.

While program description and statistics are essential tools in obtaining government funding, they are not sticky when it comes to communicating with donors and volunteers. I suggested to Dave that he tell a story at every campaign steering committee meeting to help the volunteers on the committee understand at a deeper level the work of his organization.

Need More Help From Rich? See p. 241

GREEN LIGHT
FUNDRAISING

To make the point about the power of stories to create a giving atmosphere, it's worth expanding on the story I told in the introduction. One morning in the steering committee we focused on securing the lead gift of $10,000, a gift larger than the total gifts the organization had ever raised in a single year. I explained the role of a lead gift in a successful campaign and asked the volunteers to return to the next meeting with a list of three or four people they knew who had the ability to give at that level.

At the end of the meeting Dave told a story that I referred to in the introduction. A grandmother had come to him a few days before asking for help. Her son had gotten a young woman pregnant and then broken up with the young woman. "I make no apologies for my son," said the grandma, "he was wrong to get her pregnant."

The grandmother poured out her worries about her grandson. He and his mother were living in a house with several other adults who used drugs. She was worried about the safety of her grandchild. She didn't know what to do and she came to Dave because she knew he worked for an organization that helped kids and families.

At that point in telling the story to the campaign volunteers, Dave said that his organization had a program designed to help young mothers in just this situation. It provided lots of support and teaching to young mothers on how to be good parents. This program could help the young mother move into a safer environment and learn better how to care for her son.

Unfortunately, Dave told the campaign steering committee, they had limited funding for the program and they would not be able to enroll the young mother and son until another mother completed it.

Later that day Dave called me. "Rich, you won't believe what just happened. Remember that story I told this morning at the campaign steering committee about the grandmother who was worried about the safety of her young grandson? Her grandson and his mother were living in a house with several other adults who were into drugs because she couldn't afford a place of her own.

I remembered.

GREEN LIGHT
FUNDRAISING

"One of the people at the campaign steering committee just called," Dave said, "to tell me that she wants to donate the lead gift of $10,000 and have it used to help this woman's daughter and grandson."

"I was on the interstate when she called" he continued, "and I was so shocked I almost ran in the ditch."

Stories are like the microphones of fundraising. They are a powerful way of getting your message across. They help potential donors understand and act generously.

Presenting the story

Once you've discovered the core stories of your organization, you need to present them as part of carrying out your sustainable fundraising plan. Over the years the world of marketing has developed many ways to present a company's story to potential and actual customers. There's an overlap between the worlds of marketing and fundraising.

As the internet has become a part of everyday life, marketers and fundraisers are finding new and creative ways to connect with people using the web. Ways of using the web to connect with your donors and potential donors are constantly evolving. In chapter nine we'll highlight a number of ways that you can use social media as part of presenting your story.

But first we'll focus on building the foundation for presenting your stories—the case statement.

Need More Help From Rich? See p. 241

GREEN LIGHT
FUNDRAISING

The Case Statement as Translation

The writer of a case statement not only serves as the master electrician of the document, but also as a translator. Nonprofit staff members develop a special language, often peppered with acronyms, to help them communicate effectively with each other. The special language is English but it often has meanings that outsiders cannot decipher. Here's an example, taken from a website, of insiders communicating:

Provides training (including food service) and sheltered employment to individuals with developmental disabilities to maximize or maintain their functional, social and vocational skills and to maximize their integration into the community.

The challenge for the writer of a case statement is to translate the work of the nonprofit into simple, powerful, words that can be understood by outsiders. The writer of the case statement must have the trust of insiders like the CEO and other management staff because the writer will be describing the work of the nonprofit in language that is unfamiliar to insiders. It's essential that the writer gently and firmly stick with words outsiders will easily understand despite pressure from insiders to use language familiar to them.

For instance, here's an excerpt from another website of an organization that provides similar services to the example above. See how the website writer does a great job of translating for outsiders:

Welcome to Community Support Services

Try to imagine living with a developmental disability. Imagine not being able to have a job...or have a home...or to participate in day-to-day life in your home, in your community.

Then imagine someone coming to your side and helping you remove those barriers, creating circles of support that help you to be more independent, that help you participate in the daily life that many take for granted.

That is what Community Support Services is all about.

GREEN LIGHT
FUNDRAISING

The case statement for the insiders

Simply put, the case statement presents an emotionally powerful and convincing case for raising funds through the campaign.

You can think of the process of researching and writing the statement as addressing the needs of two groups—the insiders and the outsiders. The process helps the insiders--development staff and the leaders of the organization--to think through the need the campaign addresses and how to communicate that need effectively to the outsiders—the volunteers and donors who will make the campaign a success.

Think of the work of researching and writing a case statement as similar to the work of an electrician. Much of the work of the electrician is invisible to the person who turns on the coffee maker in the morning, but without the electrician there will be no coffee aroma and no first sip.

Just as all the wires work together to produce energy when a switch is turned on, all the elements of the case statement work together to create a high-energy, powerful and convincing case for supporting the campaign.

Here are the issues the insiders need to address as background for writing the case statement:

- Clearly define the need;
- Discover the core stories;
- Show why the nonprofit is equipped to meet the need;
- Define through a budget the amount of funds needed to meet the need;
- Name all the sources of funds to be used to meet the need;
- Establish the goal the campaign needs to raise to meet its share of the funds.

The development staff and the leaders of the organization need to answer each of these issues so that the case statement writer knows the answers prior to writing the case statement.

GREEN LIGHT
FUNDRAISING

The case statement for the outsiders

Outsiders look at the case statement through a different set of eyes than do insiders. They don't have a deep knowledge of the organization like insiders and yet they want to know enough about the organization to be able to decide whether to volunteer for the campaign or donate to the organization. Let's translate the writing of the case statement in a way that donors will understand.

Clearly define the need

If you ask an executive director what he or she needs from fundraising, they are likely to respond with three words: "general operating funds." That's because executive directors are keenly aware of how much it costs the organization to provide each of its services and they want the maximum flexibility to use the funds where most needed.

But donors do not give because an organization needs money for the general fund. They give because they trust that, if they give, the organization has the ability to transform lives in a specific way through the use of the gift.

Six ways that a case statement conveys the need for gifts

1. A theme
2. Core stories of transformed lives
3. Stories as the solution to an age-old conflict
4. A campaign goal
5. Photos
6. A statement about giving to transform lives

GREEN LIGHT
FUNDRAISING

Capture the Heart through a Theme

Corporations often have tag lines that capture their purpose and passion in a few words. The best tag lines are memorable. For instance, as I was writing this, when I tried to remember corporate tag lines, I immediately thought of GE's: "Imagination at Work." Then I thought of "Like a Good Neighbor, State Farm Is There."

Corporate tag lines are designed to be memorable and to create a positive emotional response.

Nonprofits also have tag lines. Who hasn't heard the tag line for the United Negro College Fund—"A Mind is a Terrible Thing to Waste®." You may not have heard the tag line for Homeboy Industries but once you hear it, you're likely to remember it: "Nothing Stops a Bullet like a Job."

Your nonprofit may already have a tag line that you can use as the theme of your campaign. But, if your organization does not have a tag line, here are some tips for creating an effective theme.

Seven Ways to Make your Theme Sing

1. **Keep it short**--three to eight words.

2. **Use simple, concrete, memorable words.** A tag line is not the place to be abstract. History might seem abstract but see how the Montana Historical Society makes it concrete in their tag line: "Big Sky. Big Land. Big History."

3. **Capture the heart of how your organization transforms lives.** One organization I consulted with had a campaign to build an accessible house for people with developmental disabilities. Part of the core story of the campaign was that the organization had dreamed of the home for many years. In four words the theme captured the essence of the story and the purpose of the campaign: "Bringing Home the Dream."

4. **Make it emotional.** Remember, fundraising is an emotional business and you want to move people with your theme. LandChoices found a way to tap into emotion with their tag line, "Helping Preserve the Places You Cherish."

Need More Help From Rich? See p. 241

GREEN LIGHT
FUNDRAISING

5. **Make it unique.** It's tempting to borrow a theme from another campaign or another organization. Don't. You want to capture what makes your cause and campaign unique in your theme since you'll use the theme on the cover of the case statement and in news releases and marketing materials throughout the campaign.

6. **Brainstorm several possible themes.** You are unlikely to land on the winning theme on the first try. Start by filling a sheet of paper with potential themes as quickly as you can. Quickly filling a page with possible themes will force your brain to go into overdrive. As your brain goes into overdrive the potential themes you produce will range from the ridiculous to the sublime. Set the list of possible themes aside and then return later and read them again. The cream will rise to the top and you'll be able to narrow down the themes to the best three or four.

7. **Test your best themes.** Say them out loud to make sure they roll off your tongue easily. Check to make sure they meet the first six criteria for a great theme. Then test them with others. Test them with fellow staff members, board members, the campaign steering committee, and also test them with people who know little about your organization. You'll see which theme connects the best with people, and that becomes the theme for your campaign.

I am not aware of other resources devoted to writing campaign themes but Nancy E Schwartz has a great publication devoted to nonprofit tag lines. You can learn more about creating a theme for your campaign from *The Nonprofit Tag line Report: An In-Depth Survey and Analysis: Building Your Brand in Eight Words or Less* that Nancy makes available as a free download at her website, www.GettingAttention.org.

Stories from the heart of your nonprofit

If the theme is on the cover, then page one is the story from the heart of your nonprofit that portrays a life that has been transformed by the work of your organization.

Most of the time the writer of the case statement is a development staff member who does not work directly with the people served by the organization. That means you discover the core stories by talking to the staff who work with the people served by your nonprofit. You can discover the core stories by asking questions. Here are sample questions you can use with staff to uncover core stories:

GREEN LIGHT
FUNDRAISING

- Among the people you have worked with, who has made the most progress?
- Among the people you have worked, whose transformation are you most proud of?
- What approach have you used in your work that has worked really well?

As staff members tell you stories take notes and ask follow-up questions to make sure you have all the facts. Remember, you want your core stories to meet the six principles for making ideas sticky that the Heath brothers uncovered that we explored at the beginning of this chapter.

Once you have written a story, test it with the staff member to make sure you were accurate in the retelling and to make sure that it does not demean the person.

Confidentiality

The challenge the writer of the case statement often faces is to tell core stories while honoring confidentiality.

Depending on the situation, you may be able to obtain a written release from the person who allows you to use his or her name and photo.

In cases where confidentiality must be maintained, you can change the name and enough details to disguise the person's identity. When I change the name and identifying details on a story, I include a note to that effect at the end of the story.

Another challenge fundraisers face is telling stories that do not demean the person.

When I worked for an organization that served people with developmental disabilities, I tested the stories I told with staff to make sure that the stories did not demean the people we served.

Remember, integrity and compassion are the values that are the foundation of nonprofits and fundraising.

GREEN LIGHT
FUNDRAISING

Stories as Velcro for the Brain

The authors of the *Chicken Soup for the Soul* series describe stories as "Velcro for the brain." They say that concepts go in one ear and out the other but stories "Velcro" to the brain.

When you are looking for core stories from your nonprofit, consider the criteria the *Chicken Soup* authors set when they were looking for stories for their first book in the series, a collection of 101 stories. They searched for stories that produced:

1. Happy tears.
2. God bumps, goose bumps, and chilly bumps.
3. A change in perception (changing the world one person and one story at a time).
4. Weak at the knees--a story so powerful it buckles your knees.
5. Your stomach turns—the guy who has cancer and his wife and kids shave their heads
6. A new belief system emerges.
7. Smiles.
8. An awareness of new possibilities.

The *Chicken Soup* series of books has sold over 100 million copies because people are moved by the stories. Your core stories will be as powerful and will move your volunteers to ask and your donors to give generously.

Stories as the solution to an old conflict

When I first began my career in fundraising the executive director and I used to go round and round about how to present our need to donors. Many fundraisers and executive directors have had the same conflict. I wanted to raise funds for specific projects because, I argued, donors want to know how their funds will be used. If we raised funds for a specific project, then we could tell donors exactly what we accomplished with their gifts.

But my executive director was responsible for a dozen or more programs and he never

knew where the money was going to be needed. He didn't want to raise funds for one program or project and then not be able to use it for a program that unexpectedly and desperately needed the funds.

Naturally, since he was the executive director, he won the argument.

By the time I began consulting with other organizations, I had accepted the fact that executive directors need to have maximum flexibility with the funds they raise. When I developed the Green Light Fundraising system, I used stories to solve the dilemma. Rather than raise funds for a specific project or program, I had organizations raise funds by telling core stories from two or three of their programs. The stories portray an accurate picture of the approaches a nonprofit uses to transform lives.

The advantage of telling two to three stories in the case statement and in presentations is that different people will be moved by different stories.

When I met with the woman who gave the lead gift to the campaign that underwrote this book, I told stories from our work with a youth organization and a senior organization. My daughter Hannah works as the director of mental wellness for a senior program that served a metropolitan area. One day she told me within a relatively short period of time three different daughters who lived in other parts of the country called her because they were concerned about their mothers who were going through emotional difficulties. In each case, Hannah could hear the relief in their voices when she told them that she would have someone on her staff visit their mothers in their homes the next day. As I told the story I could see that this was the story that moved the potential donor the most.

Where are we headed? The campaign goal

In a political campaign everyone from the candidate to the volunteer putting up yard signs knows the campaign has one goal: elect that candidate in order to accomplish a greater good. In a fundraising campaign everyone needs to know that the goal is to raise x amount of dollars to transform lives.

The magic of a goal is that it keeps everyone moving in the same direction and whenever someone asks, "Are we there yet?" you can compare how much money

Need More Help From Rich? See p. 241

GREEN LIGHT
FUNDRAISING

you've raised with the goal. Mention the goal as many times as you need to in the case statement to make sure everyone knows where you are headed.

A picture is worth a thousand words

In addition to stories, photos of people are a powerful way to make an emotional connection. I suggest you intersperse photos throughout the case statement. Use photos to support the theme. Depending on the nonprofit you may be able to use photos of people your nonprofit serves. When I first became a development director, I taught myself how to take a good photo because I knew that photos would be an effective way of telling the stories of the lives touched by our work.

Don't use poor quality photos in your materials because it's like asking for a donation right after you've spilled coffee on yourself. It's distracting.

If you don't know how to take good photos, find a volunteer photographer.

In some cases, for confidentiality reasons, you will not be able to use the photos of people who receive services from a nonprofit. Dave McClure's organization worked with troubled youths and their families and couldn't use their photos in fundraising.

You can get stock photos online for little or no cost from http://www.sxc.hu/index.phtml. Some photos have restrictions in terms of type of use and some have requests to contact and/or credit the photographer. But with those few steps, there are thousands of great photos here, yours for the taking.

Another great source of photos is http://www.flickr.com/. Use the advance search feature to scroll down to the Creative Commons section. Click on "Only search within Creative Commons-licensed content." The advance feature allows you to search for photos that have been copyrighted under Creative Commons and are available for free as long as you follow the specific Creative Commons guidelines. The photos are tagged by topic, making it possible to search for photos by topic.

GREEN LIGHT
FUNDRAISING

A Statement about Giving to Transform Lives

When someone has read your core story in your case statement or heard it in a presentation, they will be moved and ready to act. Then it's time for the call to action; a call to give to transform lives.

Here are samples:

> *Your gift to the Youth Service Bureau of Illinois Valley will keep a family warm like the family living in a camper whose furnace went out when it was sixteen degrees below zero.*

> *Your gift to Evergreen Leaders will help us give the green light to nonprofits as we teach them a better way to raise funds for a cold day in January.*

> *Consider how your gift to the Youth Service Bureau of Illinois Valley will keep a family warm like the family living in a camper whose furnace went out when it was sixteen degrees below zero.*

How much to give

When donors have been moved by the stories of lives transformed, they want to know how much to give. They want to know how much is needed and how their gift can help. In chapter 16 on The GOOD way to ask there's a section on determining how much to ask of a potential donor. In the case statement we include a tool that quickly helps donors understand each level of giving needed to meet the goal—the gift chart.

Chapter 5 includes a section on creating a gift chart that can be used as a way of assessing the initial goal, and Chapter 12 teaches you how to use a gift chart to determine the number of volunteers needed in the advance gifts and special gifts phases. Once your organizations board and staff leaders have settled on a goal, I suggest including the gift chart in the case statement for a couple of reasons. First, it shows your donors the level and number of gifts you need to achieve the goal. Second, it can be used when training volunteers to show them the level of gifts they need to be asking for in order to have a successful campaign. Chapter 16 covers how to teach your volunteers to ask and will show how the gift chart can be used as a tool in training volunteers to ask for gifts.

 Need More Help From Rich? See p. 241
GREEN LIGHT
FUNDRAISING

Looking ahead

You've now learned how to write the heart of your case statement, the stories of transformed lives and stories of people who needed their lives transformed by the work of your nonprofit. You've learned how to translate the stories into asking for gifts to help your nonprofit transform more lives.

Now you need to learn how to include reassurances in your case statement so that your volunteers and potential donors can be confident that their gifts will be used wisely.

How can we improve?

E-mail us at (comment@greenlightfundraising.org) to let us know when something is unclear, or you have a suggestion for improving the book. Please identify the page and paragraph that needs improving.

GREEN LIGHT
FUNDRAISING

CHAPTER 8

Making The Case 102: Reassurances and Other
Case Statement Writing Tips

While stories motivate and energize donors to give to transform lives, donors also need to be reassured that the organization they are investing in is worthy. The case statement provides those reassurances in six ways:

- Knowing the organization and the campaign leaders
- Endorsements and testimonials
- A snapshot the organization's financial picture from the balance sheet
- Demographics of people served
- Accreditations, registrations and memberships
- Organizational timeline

The names and bios of the leaders

One of the most common ways that donors look for reassurance is to look at the names of the board of directors and the campaign steering committee to see who they know. If they know someone on the board of directors and have a high opinion of that person, they will feel reassured. The same goes for the campaign steering committee.

You will need to devote a page of the case statement to the organization's board and campaign leaders. List the position each holds on the board, starting with the executive committee first. Also, list the employer and position in their employer's company. Then list the campaign leaders, their positions, in the campaign, and their employer and position in their employer's company.

A truism in fundraising is that people give to people. It's also true that people are reassured by knowing and respecting the nonprofit's board and the campaign's leaders.

In addition, you may want to include the names of the executive director and key staff members and a brief bio for each, assuming that the bios establish credibility and reassure the potential donors.

GREEN LIGHT
FUNDRAISING

Endorsements and testimonials

Endorsements and testimonials are another way that donors are reassured. Donors want to hear what those who are highly respected have to say about an organization. Endorsements fill that need.

Donors also want to hear from those who have had direct experience with an organization. Testimonies fill that need. People who endorse an organization may not have direct experience with an organization but they will have high name recognition among potential donors.

Include in the case statement endorsements from community leaders, political leaders, academics, and local celebrities. Start by creating a list of people in the above categories who already have a connection to the organization through someone on the board or staff. Then add names of people in the above categories with whom you don't have a connection, but who will be well known to potential donors.

The quickest way to get an endorsement from someone who has a connection to the organization is to call them up. If you don't personally know them, get the permission of the board or staff member who has the connection to use their name when you make the call to a potential endorser. Here's how the conversation might go between Ruth, the development director who is writing the case statement, and Stan, a community leader:

"Hi, this is Ruth from the Best Nonprofit. May I speak to Stan?"

A moment later Stan comes on the phone. "Hi, Stan, this is Ruth from the Best Nonprofit. How are you doing today?"

"Fine. What can I do for you?"

"I'm in the process of writing a case statement for a fundraising campaign that we will be launching in a few months. I want to include endorsements from prominent community leaders in the case statement. George Bush, who's on our board, suggested that I give you a call."

"How's George doing? I don't see him as much since he's retired."

GREEN LIGHT
FUNDRAISING

"He's doing well. He's very active on our board which we really appreciate."

"What's this campaign about?"

"As you may have read in the paper, nonprofit's like ours are going under funding cuts from the state. We have a couple of small fundraising events each year but they only bring in about $15,000. Our board has been encouraging us to ramp up our fundraising. We've set a goal of $75,000 for our first campaign."

"That's quite a jump."

"We're using a sustainable fundraising model that's been successfully used by other community nonprofits."

"And you want an endorsement from me. What does that entail?"

"The simplest way to do it would be for you to say some positive things about Best Nonprofit and I could craft them into an endorsement and e-mail it to you for your approval. Or, if you prefer you could write 10-15 words about Best Nonprofit and e-mail it to me."

"Let's get this done right now. I'll tell you what I know about your organization. You make an endorsement out of it and e-mail to me for my approval. Best Nonprofit…"

Notice that Ruth gave Stan a choice between saying a few positive things about Best Nonprofit, which she would turn into an endorsement for his approval, and his writing the endorsement and e-mailing it to her. People prefer choices. Also, some folks think best while talking and other thinks best while writing.

Besides endorsements, testimonials are a great way to reassure donors. Testimonials come from people who have direct experience with a nonprofit and from people who have benefited from the services of the organization, donors, and volunteers. A testimonial differs from an endorsement in that a testimonial recounts personal experience.

In her blog, Getting Attention, nonprofit marketing guru, Nancy E. Swartz, published excellent articles on testimonials. Nancy has kindly given me permission to use one of the articles. Nancy covers all the key points in securing and using testimonials.

GREEN LIGHT
FUNDRAISING

Seven Steps to Compelling Testimonials for Nonprofit Organizations

Read Part One of this series at http://gettingattention.org/articles/58/branding/testimonials-powerful-marketing-copy.html

You know that there's no message more valuable than testimonials from partners, donors, members, volunteers and program participants on their experiences with your organization. Testimonials rationalize a prospect's decision to support your organization as they back up your claims and vouch for the value of your work. As a result, these unbiased words carry more credibility than anything your organization's staff has to say.

It's challenging to get the right testimonials from your network. But you can count on getting strong material when you ask this series of questions (via phone or an online survey) as soon as possible after an individual's interaction with your organization. This approach is vastly more effective than an "open mike" call for testimonials strategy.

You can ask the questions at an organization or program-specific level, depending on the messaging you're working on. Beware that asking broad questions generates broad responses that tend to be weak testimonials.

Here are the questions to ask:

1. *Why did you [join/give/volunteer with/participate in] our organization?*

This question establishes the interaction as "customer-feedback" rather than a request. A request for a testimonial is imbalanced, frequently creating a measure of tension and sometimes a resistance to responding. Customer feedback is an equal conversation; a two-way street.

2. *Please list the three things you like most about your [membership/support/volunteer work/program] and why you like them?*

Implying ownership ("your membership") personalizes the survey. Positioning this question as a positive ("like most") increases the likelihood of generating a positive response.

 Need More Help From Rich? See p. 241  GREEN LIGHT FUNDRAISING

Requesting a report back on three distinct features (for example, a program's relevance, workshop format and take-home materials) makes the respondent think hard and specifically on her response. As a result, the end product is likely to be more useful to your organization.

3. *What do you see as the most valuable aspect of your [participation/advocacy/giving to us/membership/volunteering]?*

   By asking your base to pinpoint benefits, you'll learn which ones are most important (to them and to prospects).

4. *Please tell us about any specific success that your involvement with our organization helped you achieve, and how.*

   By asking for personal experiences, you're likely to hear stories that map directly to the challenges faced by the rest of your network. Stories make information easy to relate to, and much more interesting.

5. *How has your involvement with our [organization/program] benefited you or your community in terms of increasing quality of life or satisfaction?*

   This is one of my favorite questions, leading the respondent right to the answer you're looking for. It will motivate her to tell you how your organization or program has changed her life.

6. *Is there anything about your [volunteer work/program/membership/donor communications] that you would like to see changed?*

   This question emphasizes how much you care about feedback and gives you insight into problems that need to be addressed.

7. *May we use your comments in our communications, with attribution?*

   Remember that an anonymous testimonial has far less weight that one attributed to an individual cited by name, title and organization. If you can feature her photo, all the better. That increases believability hugely! But you do need to ask her permission on all fronts.

   If you're conducting this interview via phone, send an email follow up to solicit a dated release.

GREEN LIGHT
FUNDRAISING

Polishing Testimonials for Ultimate Impact

Once you have a few testimonials in hand, move on to editing. Editing is expected, as long as you don't change the intention of the testimonial in doing so.

Here are the critical steps to take:

- *Use only the strongest testimonials you have. It's far better to have a few really good testimonials than several mediocre ones. Make sure the testimonials cover a range of benefits. Different things are important to different people. Your prospects are going to decide to get involved for different reasons. You want to cover all the main ones.*

- *Focus on a single benefit in each testimonial. Load too many in and you'll deplete the strength of the message.*

- *A length of two to three sentences works best. However, testimonials can run longer if you're telling a story.*

- *Positive messaging works best. Do edit out negative elements, such as slams on other organizations. And don't use testimonials that have an overall negative tone. They won't help your organization.*

- *Conversational is the way to go. You're bound to generate some great raw material by asking these questions. But make sure you don't overdo polishing what you get. Testimonials should be conversational in tone, just as you initially heard them. If you rewrite them formally, they'll lose their impact.*

- *Send the edited version with attribution to the source for approval, showing them exactly how it's going to look with the attribution included. Save the confirmation email you receive in return. In about 20% of cases, you'll be gifted with a revised testimonial that's even more glowing than the original.*

Need More Help From Rich? See p. 241

GREEN LIGHT
FUNDRAISING

The Good, the Bad and the Ugly

What Doesn't Work

Weak or negative testimonials are worse than no testimonials at all. Here are a few examples that add little messaging value:

> *"Imagine standing and just looking at a stainless steel 1936 Ford. It is great right? Now imagine working on it! EVEN BETTER!"*

> > *—Crawford Auto Aviation Museum Volunteer*

So what? This testimonial provides little insight to the reader.

> *"I very much appreciate all of your time and insight." (On a nonprofit news service)*

> > *—Anonymous, California, USA*

Why is that effort and insight of value? And who is speaking? If I don't know the speaker's role and organization, there's no way I can assess whether her take is relevant to me.

What Works

Here are four examples of testimonials that work, and explanations of why they do so.

> *"The best part of camp is, without a doubt, the kids – their smiles, laughter, and maturity. I volunteer to help the kids, yet I always leave camp with a renewed sense of hope and life, which comes from the kids, and what they do for their fellow campers, the volunteers, and me. In my opinion, Camp Hope is the toughest vacation you'll ever love."*

> > *—Catherine Brown, volunteer*

Catherine's articulation of all she gets from giving her time and effort is moving and motivational.

> *"They are very consistent in their pick-ups. It's very easy to arrange and I know that the things I donate will not be wasted and any money raised goes to a good cause."*

> > *—Nora C., Bridgewater, MA*

GREEN LIGHT
FUNDRAISING

Nora C. donated goods to the Big Brother Big Sister Foundation and shares the practical features (reliable pick up, easy to arrange) and more spiritual benefit (any money raised goes to a good cause) that will motivate her to do so again.

> "I credit meeting many of my career goals this year to my mentor. As a result of my mentor's invaluable coaching, I have been able to map out my job experience and determine my areas of concern, update my job application form and develop my interviewing skills."
>
> —Carolyn Ellenes

The specifics here make this testimonial a powerful one. Ms. Ellenes shares her experience in a way that highlights specific benefits (analyzing her career path and honing related skills) and value (meeting many of her career goals) of the mentoring program. We understand who she is and how program participation has made a difference in her life, making it easy for us to evaluate the relevance of this testimonial.

Finally, take a look at the Center for Media Democracy's video compilation of testimonials from members and community producers. It's three minutes of warm, fun, informational and memorable marketing, that doesn't seem like marketing at all.

Now Make Good Testimonials Even Better

It's hard to overestimate the power of a headline. Remember that today's readers skim at a fast clip. Headlines can stop them in their tracks.

Effective headlines frame a testimonial to capture attention, making content easier to absorb and increasing the potential for audiences to digest your full message. Feature a bolded headline for every testimonial (and include it when you seek permission to use the quote). Your headline should highlight the value of the testimonial, as it does in the three headline/testimonial pairings below.

Toughest Vacation You'll Ever Love

> "The best part of camp is, without a doubt, the kids – their smiles, laughter, and maturity. I volunteer to help the kids, yet I always leave camp with a renewed sense of hope and life, which comes from the kids, and what they do for their fellow campers, the volunteers, and me. In my opinion, Camp Hope is the toughest vacation you'll ever love."
>
> —Catherine Brown, volunteer

Need More Help From Rich? See p. 241

GREEN LIGHT FUNDRAISING

Easy to Arrange, Reliable Pick Up

> *"They are very consistent in their pick ups. It's very easy to arrange and I know that the things I donate will not be wasted and any money raised goes to a good cause."*

—Nora C., Bridgewater, MA

Invaluable Coaching Moved My Career Forward

> *"I credit meeting many of my career goals this year to my mentor. As a result of my mentor's invaluable coaching, I have been able to map out my job experience and determine my areas of concern, update my job application form and develop my interviewing skills."*

—Carolyn Ellenes

Used by permission.

Demographics of people served

The simplest way to reassure donors that your organization meets a significant need is through the demographics of the people you serve. Your organization probably already knows the number of people you served last year by age, sex, geographic location, diagnosis, etc. Your challenge is to not to overwhelm donors with numbers, but to pick the best numbers that portray the people served. If you can turn the numbers into easily- understood graphs, so much the better.

The balance sheet

"Donors do not," as one donor told me, "want to throw money down a rat hole." They want to know that the organization they support is on good financial footing. The simplest way to communicate this is through the balance sheet. Don't include your entire balance sheet, because only a handful of your potential donors will be able to read and understand it. Instead, pull out from the balance sheet Total Assets,. Total Liabilities, and Total Equity. This information is a simple equation, Total Assets minus Total Liabilities equals Total Equity. Note: balance sheets show the information from a specific date. Usually it's best to use the information from the last day of the most recent fiscal year. In many nonprofits that information will be available to the public through an audit.

GREEN LIGHT
FUNDRAISING

Organizational timeline

Another way to reassure donors is through a one- page organizational timeline. Depending on the age of the organization, you can choose one or two highlights per year, less if the organization is older and, more if it's younger. Limit each highlight to a sentence in length.

Accreditation, registrations and memberships

The final way to reassure donors is through recognition by external organizations. The IRS letter recognizing the organization as a 501c3 organization is the most important recognition to donors because it reassures the donor that their donation will be tax-deductible to the fullest extent of the law.

Also, list accreditations. Community nonprofits often are accredited by an organization specializing in accrediting nonprofits in their specific industry.

Last, list memberships in industry associations, United Way, Chamber of Commerce, or other memberships that will reassure potential donors.

The Rule of Three and other Case Statement Writing Tips

Very few people will read your case statement from start to finish. Fear not.

Use the rule of three developed by Marcy Heim of Heim Consulting Services (http://www.marcyheim.com/) in Madison, Wisconsin, to create a case statement that can be read three ways. Heim says prospective givers should be able to "read" the final document as follows:

- 30 seconds -- Look at the photos and large captions and get a good idea of who you are your dreams.

- 3 minutes -- Read the captions under the photos, read all the headings, maybe wander into the copy here and there and get a deeper understanding; and

- 30 minutes - Read the entire statement from cover to cover, every word.

GREEN LIGHT
FUNDRAISING

The case statement as green light

In writing the case statement you are setting up a series of green lights that can be used over and over again to keep the campaign moving. Here are three ways the caste statement will give green lights to your campaign:

Marketing green light. A well-written case statement becomes marketing gold that will be used throughout the campaign. Excerpts can be used in news releases, press packets, a brochure, public service announcements, blogs, e-letters, direct mail appeals, grant applications, and other marketing pieces. We'll go into more detail in chapter nine.

Recruiting green light. The case statement also becomes gold in recruiting campaign leadership and training volunteers. Sustainable fundraising depends on volunteer leaders and solicitors. Naturally, when someone is considering volunteering they want to know about the organization and the campaign. Volunteers, especially those in key leadership positions in the campaign, will want to assess the likelihood of success. No one wants to lead an unsuccessful venture. The case statement will provide for them explicit information on the organization and the campaign. On an implicit level, since the case statement is well-written and well-designed, it will give the message that the staff support team for the campaign knows what it is doing.

Volunteer training green light. Sustainable fundraising depends on volunteer leaders and solicitors. Since many of the campaign volunteer leaders and solicitors will be new to your organization, you need to teach them your cause. The case statement becomes the basis for training volunteers to be passionate about how your organization transforms lives and the role the campaign has in supporting the work of the organization. In chapters 16 and 17, we'll go into more detail on how to train volunteers in the cause and the art of asking for gifts during the advance and special gifts phase kickoffs.

Not by Committee but by One Writer

You now know the pieces of a case statement. Now it's time to write and rewrite the case statement until it shines. I encourage one person to be the writer, not a committee. Prose written by committee tends to use the language of the insiders and tends to be abstract.

GREEN LIGHT
FUNDRAISING

With one person as the writer, who knows his or her role is to be the translator of the language of insiders to the language of outsiders, the case statement will have flow, making it captivating and easy to understand for people without a lot of knowledge of the organization and its work.

While I advocate a single writer of the case statement, the writing will be strengthened by getting feedback from several readers both inside and outside the organization.

First, they'll catch the typos.

Second, insiders will help you make sure you accurately represent the organization and the people served.

Third, outsiders, from your marketing committee, for instance, will give you feed back on whether or not you've done a good job of translating to outsiders the language of the insiders. Simply give each a copy and ask them to write in corrections, indicate any places that are unclear, and indicate the places that they really liked. Tell them to make a check mark in the margin wherever they made a correction or comment so that you can quickly find their comments and corrections.

Where do you start writing?

To begin writing the case statement, download the Word document case statement template from the Green Light Fundraising website at http://greenlightfundraising. org/downloads/case.doc.

Go through the template and identify all the items you will need to collect and assemble the case statement, ranging from the stories of lives transformed at the heart of your nonprofit to your organization's balance sheet from the end of your last fiscal year.

Once you have assembled all of the pieces, you are ready to begin writing. Start with the part of the case statement that sounds the most fun to write. It might be the timeline of your organization or it might be the stories. Start with the most fun part because that will give you a success and build momentum for the writing of the rest of the sections.

Need More Help From Rich? See p. 241

GREEN LIGHT
FUNDRAISING

Write the first draft of the case statement with the same approach that you wrote term papers in college. Did you do your research and then write the paper during an all-nighter the night before it was due? Research and write your case statement the same way. Did you have your college papers done a week ahead of time? Write the case statement the same way.

Designing the Case Statement

Once the case statement is written, you need to think about design. In designing a case statement, you need to adapt a design that fits both the organization and potential donors. If the design is too slick, some donors will think the organization is wasting money on its fundraising materials. If the design is too drab, donors will likely think the organization does not do quality work with the people it serves.

Look at the fundraising materials used by the best fundraising nonprofits in your community. Their materials will give you an idea of what type of designs work well in your community.

You may decide to design the case statement in-house to keep costs down. You can find Word templates online that can be adapted. Also, see if you can find a designer in your community who can give you tips. You can also check out Seth Godin's web page full of design resources: http://www.squidoo.com/become-a-really-good-graphic-designer. Since I am not a good designer and don't want to spend the time to learn to be a good designer, I prefer to use the services of a professional designer.

After reading these two chapters on writing the case statement, you may feel a little intimidated. It may seem complex. Simplify it by writing one section at a time.

You may be wondering if the sections of your case statement need to be in the exact order as they are in the template. The stories of transformation are the heart of your case and need to be the first thing that readers see. You can use your best judgment regarding the sequence the remaining sections.

What if you don't have a talented writer on staff?

You may not have a person on staff who can write a great case statement. In that case, you may need to hire a talented writer in your community, or you may need to hire a fund raising consultant for this piece of the campaign. This chapter provides you with all the information you need to provide a freelancer or consultant to do the job for you.

GREEN LIGHT
FUNDRAISING

Have fun writing, and if you can't have fun writing, have fun getting it done through a freelancer or consultant.

Remember, as you create the case statement, you are creating a series of green lights for the campaign. When you write other marketing materials like news releases, direct mail appeals, and much more, you have a green light to use anything in your case statement that works for that piece.

When you train your volunteer leaders and volunteer solicitors in your cause, and in asking for every gift that will take you over the top of your goal, your case statement will make the training as easy as driving through a green light.

Looking ahead

You've now learned how to write the case for your sustainable fundraising campaign. Now you need to learn how to take the story of transformed lives to the world. In the next chapter,, you will learn how to take your message to the world through established media channels and by creating your own social media channels.

How can we improve?

E-mail us at (comment@greenlightfundraising.org) to let us know when something is unclear, or you have a suggestion for improving the book. Please identify the page and paragraph that needs improving.

GREEN LIGHT
FUNDRAISING

CHAPTER 9

Marketing: Taking Your Story to The World

My first fundraising job was in a community where the daily newspaper, the dominant AM news and sports station, and an FM music station were all owned by the same family. The family had entered the local media market in 1946. One year, in the early 1990's, the current head of the family enterprise decided to turn the business over to his son who had just graduated from college. He was the third generation to own and manage the business.

When the young man took the helm, my fundraising colleague, Jack Domagall, made a brilliant move. He called up the young man and welcomed him to his new post and asked if he could arrange a tour of our nonprofit with our executive director.

The young man agreed to the tour, and by the end of the tour, he was captivated by what a difference our nonprofit was making in the lives of adults with developmental disabilities. That tour proved to be the beginning of a relationship between our nonprofit and this key figure in the local media world.

My colleague, who was building a relationship with the young publisher of the daily, arranged for me to send news releases directly to him. As the primary PR person for our nonprofit, I soon discovered that if I wrote an excellent news release and took a good photo, the article appeared in the paper with little or no changes. At the time, we had a newsletter for our nonprofit called the Horizon Sun. So many of our press releases began to appear in the newspaper, that its own reporters joked that it was the Sun.

Once we created a relationship with the owner of the local newspaper and dominant radio stations, we had a friend who proved extremely valuable in taking our story to our world.

The friendly way to get out your story

The challenge you face as a development director is to market your nonprofit and campaign in your community in the most friendly way possible. This chapter covers six ways to communicate in a friendly manner with your donors and potential donors:

 Need More Help From Rich? See p. 241  GREEN LIGHT FUNDRAISING

- Captivating marketing with the help of a marketing committee;
- Researching local media channels;
- Building pre-kickoff awareness;
- Three steps to creating a speakers bureau;
- Six ways to be a great friend of the media;
- Creating your own media as part of your campaign:
  - Using Facebook
  - Your website
  - Create a YouTube channel
  - Your nonprofit's newsletter or e-letter
  - Creating a campaign e-letter.

What's the friendly way to get out the stories of how your nonprofit transforms lives? The friendly way means communicating in the same channels that your constituents already use.

The media world has changed from the 1990's, when radio, TV and print journalism were the primary ways for nonprofits to connect with constituents. With the advent of the internet and, more recently, social media, nonprofits have many new ways of connecting with donors and potential donors.

The internet and social media are the exciting new ways that nonprofits are connecting with the constituents. Social media is new enough that in most nonprofits it's still in the infant stage. Later in this chapter, we'll give you resources that can help your nonprofit catch the social media wave .

In the meantime, while social media is new and exciting, in order for you to find the friendly ways to get your story out to your world, your marketing plan for your campaign needs to be based on a simple question:

How do your donors and potential donors, currently access news, information and stories in your community?

GREEN LIGHT
FUNDRAISING

With the answer to that question, you can develop a plan for communicating in ways your donors and potential donors find friendly. To assist you in answering that question and building you marketing plan, it's helpful to create a marketing committee.

Captivating Marketing with the Help of a Committee

To help you develop a creative and captivating marketing plan, it's helpful to recruit three to five of the best marketing minds in your community to help you put together the marketing plan for your campaign. You can draw from people who work at marketing firms and media outlets in your community. Your executive director and the campaign chairperson can be helpful in identifying and recruiting the chairperson and members of your committee.

Four steps to marketing committee success

When recruiting the marketing committee, you need a clear description of their its role. The marketing committee creates and oversees a public relations plan using a four-step process:

1. Identify the current traditional and social media channels by which your donors and potential donors, currently access news, information and stories in your community;

2. Identify creative, cost- effective means for special gifts prospects to encounter the story of your nonprofit and campaign three times during the week of the kickoff;

3. Review and strengthen the case statement, the principle training tool for volunteer leaders and solicitors. (See Chapters 7 and 8); and

4. Create excitement for the special gifts volunteer solicitors through the media blitz.

Members of your marketing committee are going to want to know the time commitment they are being asked to make. We suggest doing the work in three to four one-hour meetings. To use the marketing committee time effectively, you will need to plan the meetings well with the chairperson of the committee.

Need More Help From Rich? See p. 241

GREEN LIGHT FUNDRAISING

We recommend you build the marketing plan based on the philosophy of Ken Kragen. Kragen started his career by managing some of the world's most important entertainers, including Kenny Rogers, Lionel Richie, Trisha Yearwood, Olivia Newton John, The Bee Gees, Burt Reynolds, The Smothers Brothers and many others.

In addition to his work in the entertainment world, he was the creator and organizer of "We Are the World,", "Hands Across America", and Cisco System's "NetAid.".

According Kragen, the most effective way to generate major public awareness is to plan three distinct public relations events to occur within a one week period of time. Kragen defines events:

- Events are something special or unique;
- They're founded on real substance;
- They capture people's imagination and attention.

In chapter 6, we covered creating a budget for the campaign. An essential element of the overall budget is the marketing budget, since your marketing committee will want to know how much you can spend on the plan. You can find an Excel spread sheet with the budget template, including the campaign portion of the budget, on the Green Light Fundraising website at http://greenlightfundraising.org/downloads/budget.xls.

Another advantage of a marketing committee is that they may be able to contribute the resources of their firms in helping to carry out the marketing plan that they help you develop. The marketing committee will be responsible for developing and executing all plans covering general information and publicity. The plans of this committee must be in harmony with the general plans of the campaign.

In creating your marketing plan, use both internal and external resources. By internal resources we mean your newsletter, website, e-letter, and any other channel of communications that you have created to reach your supporters. By external media, we mean media that is owned and operated by others in your community.

GREEN LIGHT
FUNDRAISING

Research local media channels

While your marketing committee will have a good idea of the media channels in your communities, you should do your homework. Before the marketing committee brain storm session, do your own research of the local media.

1. Newspaper

   Analyze your newspaper section by section to determine which sections are likely to be open to stories or information about the campaign. Determine reporters or columnists most likely to be open to your press releases or pitches for a story or series. Remember that your goal is to get out the stories of how your organization transforms lives. By far the best is to have the reporter write the story, because it will likely get better play.

   If you are going to pitch a story to a reporter, line up potential interviews ahead of time. If you are going to have the reporter interview someone whose life was transformed by your nonprofit's work, be sure to get releases signed ahead of time. You may also arrange for the reporter to interview your executive director and campaign chairperson.

   Remember, in order to pitch the story, you need to think of the angle ahead of time you. Your marketing committee can help you develop the hook for a story.

2. TV stations

   Analyze each news program and interview program at your local television stations to determine which will likely be open to your pitch for a story or an interview with your executive director.

3. Community websites

   Today, TV, radio and newspapers usually have websites also. Often, the sites echo content from their original media; i.e. a story from the newspaper will also appear online. But check out these sites in your community to see if they have additional sections that provide opportunities to tell your story. For instance, a newspaper may use video clips on their website. There are also may be independent websites or blogs in your community that provide opportunities to tell your story.

Need More Help From Rich? See p. 241

GREEN LIGHT
FUNDRAISING

Build pre-kickoff awareness

Your marketing plan using internal media should start ahead of time. You want your current supporters to be well aware of the campaign ahead of time.

Your marketing plan should also include plans to promote the campaign before the big public kickoff.

For instance, you will want to send a news release to the local media outlets announcing the selection of the campaign chairperson. The selection of the campaign chairperson, who is a well-known figure in your community, is a great opportunity to introduce the campaign to the community through local media.

In addition, when you secure the lead gift, you have another opportunity to publicize the campaign in local media.

Here is a table of the opportunities for sending out news releases prior to the big public relations push of the special gifts week:

MONTH	NEWS RELEASES
	Announcement of Campaign by the executive director and/or board president
	Appointment of General Chairperson Chairman Picture
	Appointment of Advance Gifts Chairman Picture
	Appointment of Special Gifts Chairman Picture
	Appointment of Marketing Chairperson
	Lead gift donor Picture

GREEN LIGHT
FUNDRAISING

Three Steps to Creating a Speakers Bureau

Speaking to groups in your community is a powerful way to get your story out to your world.

Every community has service clubs like Rotary, Lions, Kiwanis, Optimists, etc. Many communities have professional women's organizations. Every community has church groups. All of these groups need speakers. Each offers a great opportunity to tell your story. In these settings, you can open it up for questions at the end of your presentation, making it possible to see how your organization is perceived by your community.

Here are three steps to creating a speakers bureau:

1. Determine the great speakers associated with your organization.

   Most likely that will include your CEO. Others may be a board member, your campaign chairperson, or a staff member. People whose lives have been transformed by the work of your nonprofit are another great source of speakers. While someone who has received services may not be ready to speak to organizations on their own, they can team up with another speaker to make a powerful presentation. Another advantage of having several speakers is that in the special gifts kickoff week, you can have speakers at several organizations in the same week.

2. Schedule speaking engagements.

   Depending on the organization, they may schedule speakers up to a year ahead of time. You want approach the person in charge of a program well ahead of time if you are trying to schedule speakers for the week of the special gifts kickoff. You also want to choose organizations that have members who are donors and potential donors. If you choose to have speakers give presentations during the special gifts kickoff week, make sure they have members who will be approached by special gifts volunteers.

3. Create a script for speakers.

   Remember, you want speakers to tell stories of transformed lives. Many executive directors are used to describing the programs and statistics of their nonprofit. To captivate an audience you need captivating stories. Tell stories of the people who need the service of your nonprofit. And tell stories of people whose lives were transformed by your nonprofit. Use stories from the case statement.

 Need More Help From Rich? See p. 241 GREEN LIGHT FUNDRAISING

How to be a great friend of the media

One of your essential roles as a development director is to be a friend to the local media. Stop and think about it for a minute. Newspapers, radio, TV and emerging local news websites are under pressure every day to fill space and time within their media with quality news and stories that inform and entertain their audiences. At the same time, they are often inundated with news releases. If you are a friend of the media, your news releases and phone calls will rise to the top like cream.

Here are five ways you can be a friend to people in the media:

1. Don't waste reporter's time.

   Reporters are busy and they'll love you if you don't waste their time. Study the media outlet ahead of time to know how your news or story fits the publication. You want to know how your story will fit within their format. Newspapers have reporters who are assigned to sections. Don't waste the time of a reporter by trying to submit a news release to the wrong reporter or pitch an interview to the wrong program director.

   Also, lots of community newspapers will publish photos of donations being given to a charity. Know the newspaper's policy on the size the donation needs to be to qualify for a photo.

2. Consistently send out great news release.

   Since reporters are busy, you want to make their work as easy as possible. That begins with writing a great news release every time. Let's start with the basics—the standard format for a news release. Since your news release will be competing with a deluge you do not want it scream amateur, which is the surest way to get it thrown into the waste basket without being read. Write your news releases to conform with the standard news release format. See Appendix C for a guide to writing a great news release.

   Have someone proof your news releases before they go out. I've spent my career writing but I still need someone to proof my writing to catch the typos and the occasional awkward sentence. Typos make you look like an amateur and the media love to work with professionals.

GREEN LIGHT
FUNDRAISING

3. Submit great photographs.

For better or for worse, a picture is worth a thousand words. A great photo says great things about your nonprofit and the work it does.

Likewise, one poor photo is worth a thousand poor words about your nonprofit. No photos are better than poor photos. You want every picture you use to say great things about your nonprofit and the work it does.

When I first started doing public relations for a nonprofit, I taught myself how to take a good photograph. I went to the library and checked out several books on how to design a good photo. This was before digital photography. One of the tricks I learned was to shoot lots of photos to get one good one. It was not uncommon for me to shoot three rolls of 36 shots to get one good photo.

When you are shooting the presentation of a check you can shoot several photos before your subjects become restless. Shoot as many as your subjects will tolerate. The larger the group in the photo, the more shots you need to take in order to get one photo with everyone's eyes open and to make sure an important donor or volunteer does not look like an idiot. Now, with digital cameras, you can review your shots immediately to make sure you have at least one good one.

When you are shooting action photos of someone at work, or a conversation between staff and an individual, shoot 100 shots if you can from a variety of angles. You often need to take many shots to get one with just the right expressions. That way you'll increase the likelihood that you'll get that memorable photo that everyone will love.

Pay attention to the background of the photo. The background can be cluttered or it can accent the photo. Accent is better than clutter, although clutter can be removed through Photoshop. With digital photography, you can crop and touch up photos. Learn to use Photoshop or similar software to touch up your photos.

When you get a newspaper to commit to doing a feature story, they may often send a photographer as well as a reporter. That's great.

Need More Help From Rich? See p. 241

GREEN LIGHT
FUNDRAISING

You may be able to find a volunteer photographer in your community who would love chance to build his or her portfolio by shooting for your nonprofit. Or an accomplished pro may make an in-kind donation to the campaign by shooting photos.

Make sure each of your photos say a thousand wonderful words about your nonprofit.

4. Be organized.

Reporters will love to work with you if you always have your ducks in a row. When you arrange an interview, make sure the interviewee is on time.

When you arrange for someone who receives services from your nonprofit to be interviewed or photographed, make sure the releases are signed ahead of time.

5. Be personable.

6. To be a friend to reporters, you need to be more than a professional who makes their work easier. Be friendly, personable, and someone reporters enjoy working with. My colleague, Jack Domagall, was great at cracking jokes with everyone including reporters. People loved doing things for him because he was fun to be with.

7. Send a thank you note to a reporter after she or he has worked with you. People in the print media make their e-mail addresses available after each story they do. The e-mail addresses for radio and TV reporters are available on their websites. They are used to getting a lot of complaints. Surprise them and sent them a positive note after they've done a good story totally unrelated to your nonprofit.

Creating your own media

For many years nonprofits have created their own media in the form of newsletters, annual reports, and videos aimed at communicating with their supporters.

With the advent of the internet, the variety of ways that nonprofits can communicate with their supporters has expanded like the ivy on the walls of Wrigley Field where the Chicago Cubs play. And the cost of communicating with supporters via the internet has decreased like the hopes of Cubs fans in September.

GREEN LIGHT
FUNDRAISING

Nonprofits now have the opportunity to create channels of communication to supporters with little or no cost.

Facebook as part of your campaign

For the first time, the week ending March 13, 2010, Facebook surpassed Google in the USA to become the most visited website for the week. That's important news, not only in the online world but also in the nonprofit world.

As I write this my oldest friend on Facebook just turned 79, and the youngest, a niece, just entered her teen years. Given the widespread enthusiasm for this website, many of your donors and potential donors are on Facebook. Use of Facebook is sweeping the nonprofit world in the same way as it has the rest of us.

Facebook began as a way to connect with your friends but Facebook wants to make money and, as result, they are making their site friendly to businesses and nonprofits as well as individuals. Given its popularity, I suggest, that, if you decide to use a social media site for your nonprofit and your campaign, choose Facebook.

There are literally hundreds, perhaps thousands, of social media sites (like Twitter, MySpace, Flickr, etc.) that you could use as part of your campaign marketing plan. Remember the Kiss principle: Keep it simple, sweetheart. I suggest that you start with Facebook, and when you've mastered Facebook, then consider other social media avenues.

While Facebook is unlikely to replace your nonprofit's website, it has features that make it a powerful platform to connect with your donors and potential donors (as well as your volunteers), because many of them are already using it in their personal lives, and some may be using it for their businesses.

How can you use Facebook to reach your volunteers, donors and potential donors with the story of your nonprofit and campaign?

Need More Help From Rich? See p. 241

GREEN LIGHT
FUNDRAISING

Six ways to use Facebook to tell your story

1. Create and maintain an official Facebook Page.

   When you create an official page you can incorporate the name of your nonprofit into the Facebook url. Incorporating your nonprofit's name into the url will increase the likelihood that your supporters will find your fan page through Google and other search engines. Your url can be http://www.facebook.com/yournonprofitsname.

   Caution. Facebook recommends that nonprofits use the Causes application, which allows your donors to donate online to your nonprofit through Facebook. Causes was not created by Facebook, but by an independent firm that partners with Network for Good to provide this service. You can also put a link to your website's donate page on your Facebook page. I'm cautious about fundraising through Facebook or Twitter because the donations tend to be small. Social media is a variation on direct mail fundraising. Remember, if you want to raise a little money, send a letter (or use social media). If you want to raise more money, make phone calls. If you want to raise a lot of money, sit down face-to-face.

   The one time I recommend using online donations is when a donor has been solicited face-to-face and prefers to make the gift online.

2. Post photos on your official Facebook page.

   "Photos consistently get the highest engagement rate," says Randi Zuckerberg who works with nonprofits as part of the marketing team of Facebook.

   There are two ways to use photos and captions on your fan page.

   First, tell the stories of transformed lives through photos and captions. At the time of this writing, the REDF website (http://www.redf.org/) has a great example of effectively using photos and captions to tell their story. Using the practices of venture philanthropy, REDF (formerly The Roberts Enterprise Development Fund) carries out its mission to create "job opportunities through support of social enterprises that help people gain the skills to help themselves." See how they effectively use photos and captions to tell the stories of how their mission transforms lives:

GREEN LIGHT
FUNDRAISING

- Photo of a young man in a chef hat with the following caption: "Gary used to rely on the soup kitchen. Now the kitchen relies on him."

- Photo of a handsome middle age man: "David used to sleep on the doorstep. Now he runs the building."

- Photo of smiling young man: "Stephen went from public assistance to helping the public."

- Photo of young woman with a shovel: "Paula builds playgrounds for kids. And she's building her resume."

Second, shoot photos of your campaign volunteers: The only thing people love more than looking at a photo is looking at a photo of themselves or people they know. Take advantage of this by posting great photos of your volunteers. Create captions that recognize and honor your volunteers.

3. Post videos.

With the advent of YouTube, your supporters are likely to be used to seeing videos that are not highly produced. Even Bill Clinton posts videos on his Clinton Global Initiative Facebook page where he speaks directly into the camera with the only production being the Clinton Foundation logo and web address in the background over his right shoulder.

Find people in your organization—staff members, board members, persons receiving services, and volunteers--who can tell great stories about your organization. Interview them and capture them telling the story of a life transformed by your nonprofit and post them on your organization's fan page.

For more information on using YouTube, see the section below on "Create a YouTube Channel to Tell Your Story."

4. Develop a strategy for use of your wall.

Nonprofits like the Red Cross post updates on their own wall and fans interact by making comments on their wall posts. They use their wall updates in a number of creative ways:

Question to engage fans. During National Volunteers Week, they asked, "What's your most rewarding volunteer experience?"

Link to blog post. The provided a link to the blog on their website that had an update on their post-earthquake work in Haiti.

Link to story by media. They provided a link to an article in Wired on their work in Haiti.

Thanks. They thanked their fans for becoming part of their community.

News. They described what they were doing. For instance, they "released $50,000 from our International Response Fund to help families affected by the earthquake."

5. Post stories to Notes.

If you do not have a blog on your nonprofit's' website, you can use the Notes feature on your fan page to create a blog. Your most recent post to Notes will always appear at the top.

You can post stories on your blog from your case statement, newsletter, e-letter, as well as original stories on your official page.

6. Use Insight as the scorecard for your official page.

Just as Google Analytics helps you track the traffic to you website, Insight helps you understand and increase the traffic to your fan page. Insight, available to the official Facebook page administrator, gives you a ranking score of 1-5 that measures how well people are engaging with you fan page. Engagement is based on the number of fans you have, how many people are commenting, and how many people like your posts. The higher your engagement score, the better.

GREEN LIGHT
FUNDRAISING

Insight will also give you a detailed report on the demographic and geographic breakdown of people visiting your site. The report will give you feedback on your effectiveness in promoting your organization's Facebook page. For instance, after you do your special gifts kickoff, an opportunity to promote your nonprofit's page, you should see a spike in people coming to your page.

Who will manage your official Facebook page?

In addition to developing your strategy, you need to decide who in your nonprofit will be doing the posting. Social media tools like Facebook are easy to use and easy to misuse. I suggest one person do the posting, such as the development director, or a small team of two or three people. If you work as a team, you can work together to plan the content and divide the content topics so that you overlap topics.

When and how often will you post new material? Shabbir Imber Safdar and Shayna Englin analyzed nearly a year's worth of data from the UNICEF-USA Facebook page and wrote a free ebook,"Is Your Nonprofit Facebook Page Worth It?" describing their findings. Here are three nuggets from the book that were posted on the NTEN blog:

1. Clickthrough rates spikes on Wednesdays and is most sluggish on weekends.

2. Except in the immediate aftermath of a disaster, clickthrough rate drops off when UNICEF-USA posts to their fan page more than 3 times per day.

3. Clickthrough rates skyrocket during disasters, providing the best possible opportunity for fundraising.

Keeping up with advances in using Facebook for your nonprofit

Facebook is ever- changing, and nonprofits are continually coming up with new ways to use Facebook that you can adopt for your nonprofit and your campaign. Here seven online resources that you can use to keep up with the world of nonprofits on Facebook:

1. John Haydon: Discussing social media marketing for non-profits.

   Facebook is constantly tweaking its site and John is on top of it. John blogs (http://www.johnhaydon.com/) a lot of "how-tos" for nonprofits who use Facebook. I especially like that he includes screenshots, making it possible for you to see exactly what he is talking about.

GREEN LIGHT
FUNDRAISING

2. Getting Attention: Helping nonprofits Succeed Through Effective Marketing.

   Consultant Nancy E. Schwarz covers all aspects of nonprofit marketing, including using social media on her Getting Attention blog (http://gettingattention.org/). (See Chapter 8 for her advice on testimonials).

3. "Non-Profits on Facebook" page.

   Check out Non-Profits on Facebook (http://www.facebook.com/nonprofits?ref=mf). Click on their "Get Started" tab and you'll learn to Build a Presence, Engage Your Audience, Spread Your Message and much more. Click the "Like" button on the Non-Profits on Facebook page to keep learning as nonprofits evolve in their use of Facebook.

4. "Nonprofit Technology Network" page.

   NTEN has an official page on Facebook (http://www.facebook.com/nten.org). According to the info tab on their fan page, "NTEN is the membership organization of nonprofit professionals who put technology to use for their causes. NTEN is a community of peers who share technology solutions across the sector and support each other's work.

   "We enable our members to embrace advances in technology through knowledge sharing, trainings, research and industry analysis. NTEN helps you do your job better, so you can make the world a better place."

   Click the "Like" button on the Nonprofit Technology Network's Facebook page. The NTEN page is a good place to keep learning from a group that keeps nonprofits up to date on how to use Facebook effectively.

5. Facebook Best Practices

   The DIOSA Communications website has a section on Facebook Best Practices for Nonprofit Organizations (http://www.diosacommunications.com/facebookbestpractices.htm). It's contains an excellent set of "how-tos" for using Facebook for your nonprofit.

GREEN LIGHT
FUNDRAISING

6. Social Media for Nonprofit Organizations, a group on Linkedin.

Facebook keeps improving its site and nonprofits keep improving how they use Facebook. Social Media for Nonprofit Organizations on Linkedin (http://www.linkedin.com/groups?mostPopular=&gid=1172477) has a dedicated group of members who share information on how to use Facebook for your nonprofit. Join Social Media for Nonprofit Organizations and keep up with the latest ways to use Facebook as part of your marketing plan.

7. Mashable: The Social Media Guide

Mashable (http://mashable.com/) is the world's largest blog focused exclusively on Web 2.0 and social media news. While not exclusively devoted to nonprofits, it is a great resource on social media. Click on the Facebook Guidebook (http://mashable.com/guidebook/facebook/) tab and you'll find several dozen articles from beginner to advanced usage of Facebook, including "How Charities Are Finding The Good With Facebook Pages."

Create a YouTube channel to tell your story

If a picture is worth 1,000 words, a video must be worth 10,000 words.

When I directed my first major fundraising campaign in the early 1990's, we spent nearly $3000 hiring a video firm to shoot and edit a four minute film. Our executive director used the video when he spoke to several dozen community and church groups.

With the advent of digital video cameras, inexpensive video editing software, the internet and YouTube, the world of video for nonprofits has changed drastically. Now, nonprofits can tell their stories through inexpensive videos and distribute them widely and freely over the internet.

YouTube, the dominant video hosting site on the internet, has a nonprofit program (http://www.youtube.com/nonprofits) designed specifically for nonprofits in the USA, UK, Canada, and Australia. The program allows 501c3 organizations to set up their own channels on YouTube. The program excludes nonprofits that are religious or political in nature, those that focus primarily on lobbying for political or policy changes, as well as commercial organizations, credit-counseling services, donation middleman services, fee-based organizations, universities, and nonprofit portals.

 Need More Help From Rich? See p. 241
GREEN LIGHT FUNDRAISING

If your nonprofit is eligible, the YouTube program provides some excellent benefits:

- Premium branding capabilities and increased uploading capacity

- The option to drive fundraising through a Google Checkout "Donate" button

- Listing on the nonprofit channels (http://www.youtube.com/channels?s=mv&t=a&g=7) and the nonprofit videos (http://www.youtube.com/videos?s=mp&c=29) pages

- Ability to add a call-to-action overlay on your videos to drive campaigns

- Posting a video opportunity on the YouTube Video Volunteers platform to find a skilled YouTube user to create a video for your cause.

- You can also include links to videos in your newsletter.

Here's how YouTube describes the basics of effective use of videos by nonprofits:

- Reach Out. Post videos that get YouTube viewers talking, and then stay in the conversation with comments and video responses.

- Partner Up. Find other organizations on YouTube who complement your mission, and work together to promote each other.

- Keep It Fresh. Put up new videos regularly and keep them short—ideally under 5 minutes.

- Spread Your Message. Share links and the embed code for your videos on your Facebook page so your supporters can help get the word out.

- Be Genuine. We have a wide demographic, so high view counts come from content that's compelling, rather than what's "hip."

GREEN LIGHT
FUNDRAISING

Using your nonprofit's website to tell your story

Here's the central question to determine how much you can use your nonprofit's website to promote your nonprofit and campaign: "How much traffic does your website currently have?"

If your website is like a brochure, providing information that is not frequently updated, then the traffic to your site is likely to be slow.

In determining whether your website can be an active media channel for your campaign, you need to determine how your website was created. Was it created using a content management system (CMS)? A CMS is designed to be updated easily and, if your website was created using a CMS, hopefully you are updating it regularly. There are two, free open source content management systems, Joomla and Drupal, that many nonprofits use. WordPress is also evolving into a CMS and some users find it easier to use than Joomla and Drupal.

If your website was not created using a CMS, you need to determine when and how to switch to a website based on a CMS. Smaller nonprofits are unlikely to have a web designer on staff who can design a website based on a CMS. Since it will be costly and time-consuming to move your website to a CMS-based system, you'll need to determine whether to invest the time and money to make the move.

You'll also need to determine, prior to designing a CMS-based website, how you want to use your website. If you have a website, it likely already provides basic information about you nonprofit, describing your mission, services, board, leadership, contact information, etc. With a website built on a CMS based system, you can go the second mile to use your website to engage your supporters.

Need More Help From Rich? See p. 241

GREEN LIGHT FUNDRAISING

Five Ways to Engage Supporters Through your Website

1. Use video.

   With the advent of Youtube, you can make no-cost, or low- cost videos, and design your website so that videos show up on your home page. See the section above about how to use video on your Facebook fan page. You can use videos in the same way on your web page.

2. Use a blog.

   With a CMS-based website, you incorporate a blog into your website. People will check out your website if it is updated regularly and a blog is a great way to update your website quickly and regularly. Use the blog to tell stories of transformed lives and also to honor your volunteer leaders and solicitors.

   A blog can also make your website interactive, since you can set it up so that people can comment on your blog posts.

3. Include a donate button.

   You can be assured that many of your supporters, especially your younger supporters, are used to doing much of their business online—paying bills, banking, and shopping. A donate button will make it easy for them to donate to you online. As part of training your volunteers to ask, be sure to include a section on giving online. (See Chapter 15).

4. Show your credibility on your website.

   Your donors want to know that you will use their gifts wisely. With the advent of the internet, transparency is the name of the game. Your nonprofit's 990 is a matter of public record and can easily be found online through Guide Star and other sites. To create trust with your donors, I suggest you post your 990 as well as your annual reports on your website.

5. Experts on staff: "Let me make you famous."

   My colleague, Jack Domagall, when he was recruiting someone to be part of a photo, story, or fundraising letter, would say, "Let me make you famous."

GREEN LIGHT
FUNDRAISING

You have experts on staff. Your organization specializes in transforming the lives of the people you serve, and as such, you have staff members who are experts in their fields. You can help your experts translate what they know into terms that ordinary people can understand and turn your website into a resource for people looking for helpful information. Feel free to use Jack's line, "Let me make you famous."

Here are examples to help you think about how to translate expertise into a web resource:

- Staff of a day-care could write helpful tips of child development;

- Staff of youth organization could write tips on parenting teens;

- Management staff could write tips on leading and managing a nonprofit;

- Staff of a soup kitchen could offer recipes for large groups; or

- Staff from a senior organization could write tips on grieving.

Your staff experts could write for the organization's blog, or you could develop an online resource library by topic with free pdf or Word downloads.

Newsletters and e-letters

Many nonprofits have their own newsletters that they send to donors and supporters. If your newsletter has a good readership, make it an important part of getting out the story of your nonprofit and your campaign.

With printing and postage costs increasing, some nonprofits have begun switching to e-letters. Collecting e-mail addresses from all your supporters is the big challenge to switching to an e-letter.

Evergreen Leaders uses AWeber, an e-mail marketing program for small businesses that can be easily adapted for nonprofits. AWeber has over 150 templates that you can choose from to design your e-mails. They also have excellent support. We can send up to e-mails for up to 500 addresses for $19 a month, while 5001-10,000 is $69 a month. The cost of communicating to your donors through e-mail is substantially less than through traditional mail. There are numerous other companies besides AWeber that provide e-mail marketing programs.

Need More Help From Rich? See p. 241

GREEN LIGHT
FUNDRAISING

E-letter programs also provide you with important statistical information, such as the number of subscribers, the number of e-letters opened and the number of e-letters bounced.

AWeber also provides you with the code to insert an invitation to subscribe that you can place on your website. Each e-letter also has a subscribe button so that if someone forwards your e-letter to a friend, the friend can click on the subscribe button and use the automated subscribe feature. Each e-letter also has an unsubscribe button so that your subscribers can control whether they get your e-mail. The unsubscribe button reduces the chances that the e-letter will be treated as spam by spam blockers.

You can sign up for a thirty-day trial of AWeber for $1 by clicking on the following link: http://www.aweber.com/?369499. Full disclosure. Evergreen Leaders is an affiliate of AWeber and receives a modest credit for each referral.

Create a campaign e-letter

The final advantage to an e-letter program is that you can create e-letters for sub-groups of supporters. When you are running a campaign, a weekly e-letter is an excellent way to communicate with and cheer on your volunteers. In designing your campaign e-letter, here are sections that you may want to consider:

- Photo of someone whose life is being transformed by your nonprofit, with a caption highlighting the transformation. This section can be a constant reminder of why your volunteers are volunteering.

- Progress reports on recruiting

- Photos and bios of newly- recruited volunteer leaders and solicitors.

- Progress report on movement towards goal

- Links to media stories about the campaign

- Links to stories, videos, and photos on your nonprofit's web page and organization's official Facebook page

Who is the audience for the campaign e-letter?

1. Staff.

GREEN LIGHT
FUNDRAISING

For better or for worse, your staff is marketing your nonprofit by word of mouth all the time. Every time they talk to a friend or family member about their job and the place where they work, they are marketing. When someone they know, hears about your nonprofit and the campaign, that person is going to ask the staff member about it.

One of my regrets from directing my first capital campaign is that I did not do an adequate job of keeping the staff informed from the beginning of the campaign. Consequently, staff began to follow the campaign though the grape vine.

Don't make the same mistake as I did. Let staff members know about the campaign during the planning stage, and subscribe each staff member to your campaign e-letter, beginning with the first issue. They'll be in the loop and prepared to do good word- of- mouth marketing.

2. Board.

Board members are the chief marketers for your nonprofit and your campaign. Once they approve the campaign, they are committed to its success. Their friends and colleagues know that they are on the board and look to them to have the inside scoop on your organization and campaign. Subscribe them immediately to the campaign newsletter so that they will always have the inside scoop throughout the campaign.

3. Volunteer leaders.

Other than the campaign chairperson, who oversees all aspects of the campaign, the volunteer campaign leaders each have their areas of responsibility in the campaign. They will be working hard to be successful in their domain. At the same time, they will be interested in how the overall campaign is progressing. The e-letter will give them the picture of how the whole campaign is working together to transform lives.

4. Volunteer solicitors.

Each solicitor will ask five people for gifts. But they are also your frontline marketers for the campaign, because they will be handling the questions and

Need More Help From Rich? See p. 241

GREEN LIGHT
FUNDRAISING

concerns of the people they are asking to give. Along with the case statement, the e-letter will give your solicitors the picture of how your nonprofit and the whole campaign is working together to transform lives.

Using your nonprofit's official Facebook page as part of the campaign

You can experiment with using Facebook as a way to help volunteers stay in touch with the campaign. Facebook has a variety of tabs that you could use for campaign purposes. For instance, you could post photos of volunteers and the kickoffs.

You can post a video on Facebook and put a link to the video in the e-letter.

You could also use the Notes section to post updates on the campaign.

The important part of using Facebook is to plan how you are going to use it before the campaign. You may be fortunate enough to have someone on your marketing committee with experience in creating and managing official Facebook pages to help a company connect with its customers.

Start out with a simple plan for using Facebook as part of your campaign. You can always get more sophisticated with more experience. Make sure that you have a plan that you have the time to follow.

Feeling overwhelmed?

By now, as you've read this chapter, you may be feeling overwhelmed by the number of options you have for marketing your nonprofit and your campaign. Don't worry. You don't have to use every one of these options.

I've deliberately given you lots of options because I trust you to be able to choose the ones that fit your community, your nonprofit and you.

Your market research and your marketing committee will help you identify the most productive media channels to use in your community.

GREEN LIGHT
FUNDRAISING

The final key to a workable marketing plan is to commit to those marketing channels that will be the most productive and that you can realistically see yourself and other staff carrying out. The first year of sustainable fundraising is the most challenging. You may decide to commit to fewer marketing actions the first year in order to make sure that you are able to follow through on your marketing plan. You can always add more marketing in subsequent years.

Looking ahead

A sustainable fundraising drive requires a team effort on the members of the staff most directly involved with the campaign—the executive director, the development director, and the development assistant. In the next chapter, we explore ways that you can fit together the unique talents, as well as weaknesses, that each brings to their role in the campaign.

How can we improve?

E-mail us at (comment@greenlightfundraising.org) to let us know when something is unclear, or you have a suggestion for improving the book. Please identify the page and paragraph that needs improving.

CHAPTER 10

Tapping Into The Talents of The Staff

One day, several years ago, shy, awkward Angela wandered by Plow Creek's outdoor basketball court where a group of Plow Creek kids ranging from early grade school to high school were playing a pick-up basketball game. Plow Creek is the rural religious community where I live.

"Angela, do you want to play?" one of the players asked.

"No."

"Angela, play with us. It's fun," someone said.

After a bit more urging Angela conceded. The players quickly realigned the teams in order to keep them balanced by age, size, and skill. It's not fun when one team dominates another.

Soon the ball made its way to Angela. The person who was guarding her drifted back, allowing her space, and her teammates shouted, "Shoot, Angela, shoot." Even some on the other team encouraged her to shoot.

Humble hierarchy path

Humble hierarchy leaders have little personal ambition, an unwavering will to help the organization transform the lives of those it serves, and a passion to create space for all to thrive.

The best and most innovative work comes only from true commitments freely made between people in a spirit of partnership, not from bosses telling people what to do. Leadership cannot be assigned or bestowed by power or structure; you are a leader if and only if people follow your leadership when they have the freedom not to.

— Jim Collins in Leading Beyond the Walls, a book edited and produced by the Peter F. Drucker Foundation on Non-Profit Management and published by Jossey-Bass books, 1999.

The shot clanked off the backboard, a wild miss. Her teammates got her the ball again while the other team watched. Again she shot. She shot until she had the joy of scoring in the game.

The other team took the ball out of bounds and passed it to their most competent, competitive player, who was guarded by the best player on the other team. Sweating, they battled each other.

I loved watching those games that incorporated

Need More Help From Rich? See p. 241

GREEN LIGHT
FUNDRAISING

players of diverse ages, talents and skills. I loved watching them realign the teams whenever they added someone to the game. No adult was there to be the boss. I was a cheer leader, not a coach, and the kids ran the game and played it.

As I observed the children on the court, I learned seven lessons that you can apply in your work as a fundraising leader.

You are about to become a leader in a fundraising campaign in which most of the workers are volunteers. You have none of the traditional corporate controls to ensure that people show up at meetings and follow through. Every day, volunteers are free to choose to make powerful contributions to the campaign, or simply not to show up.

Depending on how you approach the task, playing a staff leadership role in a campaign can be exhilarating or terrifying. My job is to help give you the leadership tools to make it fun, productive and gratifying.

You can think of working together on a campaign as an interesting combination of serious business, where people's lives depend on you, and child's play.

Here are the seven lessons that these children playing pick-up basketball taught me about helping groups thrive. These are simple principles that can be used to lead a campaign:

1. Groups thrive by including people with a great variation in skills, talents, and interests;.

2. It's fun to include new people;

3. As soon as someone new joins, balance the teams;

4. Make sure the newest participant scores early;

5. Basketball has a clear set of rules, but be flexible to include new people;

6. Participants quickly figure out who the experts are; and

7. The group can run the game.

GREEN LIGHT
FUNDRAISING

Campaign staff members thrive on variation in skills, talents, and interests

The number of staff members who play roles in Green Light Fundraising depends on the size of the organization. In the smallest organizations, the executive director and an assistant may be the staff team. Larger organizations may have an executive director, a development director, an assistant director, and a development assistant. In this chapter, I describe the roles of staff in a larger organization. If you have a smaller organization, you can review the three roles and reallocate them to a two-person staff team. If you have a larger organization, with more development staff, you have the luxury of dividing the roles between more people.

The most important principle in determining who plays what role is to embrace the natural variation in skills, talents, and interests present in your team.

Assign roles based on talents

In assigning roles in your Green Light Fundraising campaign, you can benefit from the research done by the Gallup Organization. According to Gallup.com, "Gallup's employee engagement work is based on more than 30 years of in-depth behavioral economic research involving more than 12 million employees." Gallup Organization asked employees hundreds of questions in search of a few good questions to measure what a work place looks like where employees are highly engaged. Eventually they were able to narrow down the questions to just 12.

Talent path

Organizations thrive by fitting together the strengths and weaknesses of individuals.

There are 12 key dimensions of great workplaces, according to Marcus Buckingham and Curt Coffman in *First Break All the Rules: What the World's Greatest Managers Do Differently.*

Need More Help From Rich? See p. 241

 GREEN LIGHT FUNDRAISING

Gallup Organization refers to the key dimensions as q12 and have show that they consistently correlate with those workgroups that have:

- Higher employee retention;
- Higher customer satisfaction;
- Higher productivity;
- Higher profits;
- And higher safety records.

While Gallup's study focused on the business world, I think we can safely assume that if they had focused on the fundraising programs of nonprofits, they would have found a correlation between fundraising programs that are great work places, and those that raise more money.

Number three of Gallup's q12 says that, "At work I have the opportunity to do what I do best every day." In dividing up the roles in your staff development team, your aim is to be able to have each team member answer the above question affirmatively.

It's surprising the number of people who cannot answer the question affirmatively. In fact, Gallup discovered that the higher people go in an organization, the less likely they are able to say, "At work I have the opportunity to do what I do best every day."

How do you assign development staff roles so that each person can answer the question affirmatively? People who get to use their talents every day, Gallup discovered, are likely to say, "At work I have the opportunity to do what I do best every day."

The Gallup Organization has done a lot of work studying people, great managers and great workplaces. I like what they have discovered about how great managers define talent:

> ...they define talent as "a recurring pattern of thought, feeling, or behavior that can be productively applied. (Marcus Buckingham and Curt Coffman in First Break All the Rules: What the World's Greatest Managers Do Differently, p. 71)

GREEN LIGHT
FUNDRAISING

You will notice that there are three parts to this definition of talent.

1. First, a talent is a recurring pattern.

   When our brain hands us a talent, it says, "I like that. Let's do it again."

2. Second, a talent can involve "thought, feeling, or behavior."

   When our brain hands us a talent it can be in the form of a recurring pattern of "thought, feeling, or behavior."

   My brain loves to read. Ever since I learned to read I've done it over and over again. By sixth grade I was reading a book a day. Wherever I go I carry a bag with magazines and books in it. I never know when I'm going to have a moment for reading.

   A few years ago, I recognized that my brain loved to read. I remember saying to a couple of friends of mine, "I'd love to have a job where I'm paid to read." She thought I was nuts. After all, whoever heard of a job that paid someone to sit around all day and read.

   After I launched Evergreen Leaders and began writing about leadership and fundraising, I realized I was being paid for that recurring behavior—reading. In order to teach nonprofit leaders and fundraisers how to help their nonprofits to thrive, I need to do what I love, read.

3. That brings us to the third element of Gallup's definition of talent--a talent is a recurring pattern of thought, feeling or behavior that can be "productively applied."

   So the question is not who will give me a job to sit around and read all day, but how can I productively apply my talent for reading? When I put it that way, it opens up lots of possibilities. There are lots of jobs that require a talent for reading: editor, writer, teacher, researcher, consultant or pastor. My current position as CEO and Teacher's Assistant for EGL productively applies my talent for reading, as well as other talents.

GREEN LIGHT
FUNDRAISING

Beginning in the 1990's the USA federal government poured a lot of money into brain research. They discovered that when a child is born she has 100 billion neurons. As soon as the baby is born, those 100 billion neurons begin to make connections like crazy with other neurons. By the time the child is three, each of those neurons has as many as 15,000 connections. Then, at age three, the brain says, "We need some order here." How does the brain create order? Between the ages of three and fifteen, the brain begins to turn some of the connections into four lane highways and lets other connections fade out.

Our brain loves tooling down the four lane highways it developed between the ages of three and fifteen. The four lane highways in our brains are our talents: "a recurring pattern of thought, feeling, or behavior that can be productively applied."

4. There will not be a perfect fit between talents and roles. The challenge is to make sure that there is a good enough fit between talents and roles so that each staff person is able to say, "At work I have the opportunity to do what I do best every day."

What does a thriving fundraising program look like?

- People know their talents.
- The workplace honors their talents.
- Everybody works together for good.

Executive director

In a fundraising campaign the executive director (sometimes titled CEO, President, etc), plays five key roles.

1. Champion of the campaign.

   The executive director is the internal and external champion of the campaign. An organization cannot adopt the sustainable fundraising model unless the executive director not only gives the green light to the campaign, but also persuades the board to give it the green light. Undertaking sustainable fundraising requires a public commitment on the part of the organization. The local media will cover the campaign and support the campaign by doing

GREEN LIGHT
FUNDRAISING

stories about the organization.

The executive director, as the most public representative of the organization, will need to be a fully- committed champion of the campaign and ready and willing to play that public representative role in the campaign. In addition to championing the campaign to the board, media and public, the executive director needs to champion the campaign to top staff. The development staff will need the help of program staff to identify the core stories to be used in the campaign case statement, and be available to be interviewed by media for stories about the organization's program. The program staff will also need to contribute to the campaign during the inner circle phase, a topic covered in detail in chapter 13. The program staff can be valuable champions of the campaign with their friends and family. They are likely to champion the campaign if the campaign is being championed to them by the executive director.

2. Champion of the Organization

The executive director champions the organization. Key campaign leaders and donors to the campaign will make commitments to the campaign because of the passion that the executive director has for the organization and the way that it transforms lives. In his or her role of champion for the organization the executive director is the chief story teller. Stories of the needs of the people served by the organization, and stories of lives transformed by the work of the organization are the best way for people to understand the work of the organization, and to make an emotional connection. I tell executive directors to tell one story at each campaign steering committee meeting. Telling stories does two things: one, it is a quick and powerful way to show a group of volunteers what the organization is about; two, it shows the volunteers and donors how important their work of fundraising is in transforming lives in remarkable ways.

Need More Help From Rich? See p. 241

GREEN LIGHT
FUNDRAISING

3. Campaign leadership recruiter

The executive director plays a key role in recruiting the top campaign leadership. The general chairperson is the most important campaign volunteer. Each community has a handful of community leaders who have the clout and stature to chair a campaign successfully. The executive director, along with the board chairperson and perhaps one or two other board members, are keys to recruiting the best chairperson.

When they meet for lunch or breakfast with a top leadership candidate, the executive director champions the organization and explains why the campaign is essential to the success of the organization. The board president or another peer of the potential recruit asks the person to take on the role of the general chairperson. Once the general chairperson is on board, the executive director accompanies the general chairperson to recruit the other top volunteer leadership posts.

4. Media representative

The executive director represents the organization to the media. Even before launching the campaign, the executive director is likely to be the "face" of the organization to the local media. Since a media blitz is an essential element of laying the groundwork for volunteers asking for gifts, the executive director will play the role of the "face" of the organization to the media.

5. Chief thank you officer

The executive director will sign all the thank you letters and hand-write notes for those donors whom he or she knows personally. In addition, the executive director will call and personally thank the top level of donors.

Development director

The development director is like the chef of a restaurant. A chef doesn't make every dish or serve every customer but she makes sure it all works together for a great experience for the customers. Likewise, the director of development makes sure that all the parts of the campaign work together to create a great experience for volunteers and donors.

She maps the campaign using a calendar that lists all the key timelines and meetings for the campaign from start to finish. (Check out Chapter 7 to learn how to map the campaign using a calendar.)

She oversees every phase of the campaign from start to finish.

She works with the campaign chairperson to develop an agenda for each campaign meeting to help the meetings to flow efficiently and effectively. She makes sure that there are minutes taken at each meeting, highlighting who is responsible for each task and the due date for each task.

She develops the marketing plan and either writes every word or arranges every word, case statement, press release, public service announcement, interview, speech, photograph, campaign e-letter, etc.

She oversees the research and development of a productive prospect list divided by levels of potential giving. (See Chapter 14)

She oversees the development of a packet for every volunteer solicitor. She oversees the training of volunteers in the cause and in asking for gifts.

She develops and implements a plan for regular e-letter updates on the campaign introducing key volunteers, telling short stories from the organization, and tracking progress for each giving phase of the campaign.

She oversees the systems to process gifts including bank deposits, entering data in the donor data base, and ensuring that each donor is properly thanked.

She oversees any special events that are part of the campaign.

And she oversees the celebration of success at the end of the campaign, making sure that all the key volunteers and donors are honored.

GREEN LIGHT
FUNDRAISING

Development assistant

Every campaign needs an organizational genius, someone who loves making all the details line up in beautiful rows. If the development director is like the chef, who makes sure it all works together for a great experience for the volunteers and donors, the development assistant is the one who loves to set a beautiful table.

The development assistant is the master of the donor database. The database is a computer program that makes it possible to keep track of donor and prospect names, home or business addresses, phone numbers, cell numbers, e-mail addresses, donations, campaign phases, and other key information, such as board memberships, interests, relationships, who is responsible for soliciting a prospect, who has given, who has been thanked, etc.

People love to have their name spelled correctly and they hate it when their father who has been dead for three years receives, a fundraising letter from a charity. The development staff team needs someone who loves to make sure that names are spelled correctly.

I once was working on a campaign brochure that had gone through several drafts with input from volunteers and other staff members. By nature, I am not a detail person. Finally, I thought, we are ready to send it to the printer. What a relief. Then my assistant said, "Wait, we haven't proofed the names." I wanted to groan but I knew she was right. We proofed the names and discovered we had misspelled the executive director's name. I shuddered. We had almost misspelled the boss's name 5,000 times. Thank goodness I had an assistant who loved to set the table beautifully.

Campaigns are built on lists. Early on in the campaign preparations, you will probably be adding names to your donor database from service clubs, country clubs, chambers of commerce, etc. Then you will have a small group of confidential volunteers review the prospect list to rate the giving potential level of each donor. The development assistant enters the giving potential of each donor into the data base and then produces lists for volunteers to choose five people to ask for a donation at the right giving level. The development assistant is lord or lady of the lists.

If the staff time is limited for the development assistant role, you can sometimes find a volunteer to take on certain parts of the role.

GREEN LIGHT
FUNDRAISING

Each phase of the campaign starts with a kickoff in which volunteers select five prospect cards, each with the information necessary to contact a prospect to ask for a gift. The development assistant uses the database to track the progress of each of the prospects who they ask for a gift.

Once a phase has been kicked off, the development assistant provides weekly reports to each phase and team leader on the progress of their phase and team. (For more details on the scorecards see Chapter15.)

The development assistant is the angel of details for the campaign.

Staff as a model for volunteers

"The best and most innovative work," says Jim Collins, best-selling author of *Good to Great: Why Some Companies Make the Leap... and Others Don't*, "comes only from true commitments freely made between people in a spirit of partnership, not from bosses telling people what to do."

A successful campaign depends on volunteers who freely commit to the campaign and to working in a spirit of partnership for a great cause. Campaigns begin with a small group of staff (and sometimes a consultant) working together. You can think of that small core of staff as the group that creates the DNA for the entire campaign. When staff members have freely chosen their roles and are working in a spirit of partnership, they create space for volunteers to do the same.

As staff members work together and grow their team through volunteers, you'll do well to remember the observations that I made as the children of Plow Creek recruited people for their basketball games:

1. It's fun to include new people;

2. As soon as someone new joins, balance the teams;

3. Make sure the newest participant scores early;

4. Basketball has a clear set of rules but be flexible to include new people;

5. Participants quickly figure out who the experts are; and

6. The group can run the game.

Need More Help From Rich? See p. 241

GREEN LIGHT
FUNDRAISING

While a sustainable fundraising campaign involves a lot of volunteers, its culture is set by the small group of staff having fun working together for a great cause.

Looking ahead

Now you are ready to learn how to recruit the two most important volunteers in your campaign.

How can we improve?

E-mail us at (comment@greenlightfndraising.org) to let us know when something is unclear, or you have a suggestion for improving the book. Please identify the page and paragraph that needs improving.

GREEN LIGHT
FUNDRAISING

CHAPTER 11

The Two Most Important Volunteer Leaders in
The Campaign

The success of your campaign depends on influencing volunteers and donors. The two most influential people in your campaign are the campaign chairperson and the person or business that gives the lead gift.

Before we look at the type of leaders who can fulfill these roles and the responsibility of each, here's a little background on six powerful principles of influence that you can use in your campaign.

Fundraising is the art and science of influencing people for your cause. Robert Cialdini, a social psychology professor at Arizona State University, has made a career out of studying how we humans influence one another. In *Influence: Science and Practice*, a book translated into nine languages, Cialdini identifies the six universal principles of influence:

1. Reciprocation. People give back to you the kind of treatment that they have received from you.

2. Scarcity. People will try to seize the opportunities that you offer them that are rare or dwindling in availability.

3. Authority. People will be most persuaded by you when they see you as having knowledge and credibility on the topic.

4. Commitment. People will feel a need to comply with your request if it is consistent with what they have publicly committed themselves to in your presence.

5. Liking. People prefer to say yes to your request to the degree that they know and like you. No surprise there.

6. Consensus. People will be likely to say yes to your request if you give them evidence that people just like them have been saying yes to it.

During the course of your campaign you will probably use all six of the principles of influence. In this chapter, we want to focus on the two most important leaders in the campaign and how they will influence others to make a success of the campaign.

GREEN LIGHT
FUNDRAISING

Leading as the campaign chairperson

The campaign chairperson should be an outstanding person--a well-known community leader, enthusiastic about the project, able to preside at meetings, and willing to devote the necessary time to help the campaign succeed. In each community, there are a handful of people who can fulfill this role.

Pre-campaign committee

How do you go about recruiting a campaign chairperson? Usually it takes influential people to recruit influential people. The first step in recruiting a chairperson is to create a pre-campaign committee whose purpose is to recruit the campaign chairperson and to assist in soliciting the lead gift. We'll focus on the lead gift later.

Your pre-campaign committee should draw from a pool of the nonprofit's most influential board members, past board members, donors, and community leaders who have a connection to the organization. From this pool, ask five or six people to serve on the pre-campaign committee. The chief executive and the development staff person should also serve on the committee. The pre-campaign committee will serve two to four months depending on how quickly it completes its two tasks—recruiting the campaign chairperson and soliciting the lead gift.

In the first year of the campaign you want to recruit the best of this handful of people in your community who have the clout to lead a successful campaign. You may not be able to recruit the best person but that's where you start. Engage the pre-campaign committee in identifying the best five or six candidates for the chairperson in your community. Potential campaign chairpersons may or may not have been involved previously with your nonprofit. If they have, good. If not, it's much more important that they be respected and influential leaders in the community. You can teach someone about your nonprofit. You don't have time in your campaign to teach someone to be a powerful community leader. You need to choose someone who already is an influential community leader.

Need More Help From Rich? See p. 241

GREEN LIGHT FUNDRAISING

Once the pre-campaign committee has agreed on the top five to six potential chairpersons, the committee then ranks them in the order that they will be recruited. The reason why you rank them—one, two, three, etc.—is because people say no. And it's very discouraging to be told no. In the first capital campaign I directed, we asked five people and it was the fifth one who said yes. If you recruit someone and the person says no, the pre-campaign committee already knows who they will recruit next.

Successful recruiting requires planning. Once you have the candidates ranked, the committee focuses on developing a plan for recruiting the person who is ranked number one. First, plan who will be part of the recruiting group. Ideally each person in the recruiting group should have a personal connection with the candidate.

Once, while doing a feasibility study, I interviewed a man who had been recruited to lead a campaign for his high school. He said that a friend of his invited him to lunch. He assumed they were meeting to talk about a fishing trip. When twelve people showed up for lunch, he began to be a little suspicious. When during lunch, all twelve told him he was the right person to lead the campaign, he accepted.

The secret to sustainable leadership

To have sustainable fundraising you need to use your volunteer leaders and not burn them out.

You do that in two ways.

First, each leader from campaign chairperson, marketing chairperson, and the chairpersons of the solicitation phases serves for only one campaign year or cycle.

Second, for each chairperson, you recruit a co-chairperson who will serve as chairperson the following year.

In summary, you sustain volunteer leadership by recruiting leaders for one year, and recruiting their replacements a year ahead of time.

GREEN LIGHT
FUNDRAISING

Recruiting at this level must be done in person, preferably at a breakfast or lunch meeting. Before I cover the steps to a successful recruiting meeting, let's cover the responsibilities of the chairperson since the person whom you are recruiting will want to know what's expected of him or her.

Responsibilities of the campaign chairperson

1. Chair the Campaign Steering Committee, the group that keeps the campaign on track from start to finish. The Steering Committee includes the co-chairperson (who will become the campaign chairperson the following year), the executive director of the nonprofit, other staff liaisons, and the chairpersons of the following:

    - Inner Circle (board, staff, volunteers)

    - Advance gifts

    - Special gifts

    - Geographic or other solicitation divisions of the campaign

    - Marketing committee

    - Prospect committee

2. Give counsel and leadership in the direction of the entire campaign.

3. Assist in recruiting chairpersons to serve on the Steering Committee.

4. Assist in soliciting the lead gift for the campaign.

5. Speak to media regarding the campaign.

6. Work with the development director to give quotes for news releases, campaign updates, the case statement, and other marketing materials.

7. Sign campaign solicitation letters and thank you letters.

You can download this model campaign chairperson role description on the Green Light Fundraising website at http://greenlightfundraising.org/downloads/chairperson.doc.

Need More Help From Rich? See p. 241

GREEN LIGHT
FUNDRAISING

The meeting to recruit the chairperson

Here are the steps to the successful recruiting meeting of a chairperson:

1. Identify who will participate.

   A combination of board members, community leaders, the executive director and development director makes the most sense; however, each situation will differ, so the pre-campaign committee will need to use their best judgment.

2. Identify the date, time and place for the meeting.

   Those on the pre-campaign committee who know the candidate best will know his schedule and can suggest a couple of dates. Likewise, they will know whether he would prefer to meet for lunch or breakfast, and his favorite restaurant for business meetings. Remember Cialdini's principle of reciprocity: People give back to you the kind of treatment that they have received from you. Arrange ahead of time for the cost of the meal to be covered by the organization.

3. Identify the best person to invite the candidate.

   We are assuming that the best person is on the pre-campaign committee. If not, the committee may take the best person into their confidence and ask that person to invite the candidate to the meeting.

4. Plan how the best person will invite the candidate.

   It's essential that the person who invites the candidate not tell the person that she or he is being recruited to be the chairperson of the campaign. The person could say, "I want to talk to you about a project I'm working on," or something along that line. The person who does the inviting has to be influential enough and liked enough by the candidate that he or she will agree to a breakfast or lunch without knowing the precise purpose. If the candidate presses to know the purpose, the person making the invitation can simply say, "Let's enjoy a meal together and we can get into the details then." The person doing the inviting will know the person well enough to develop a good approach. The purpose of this step is to make sure the person has an approach in mind before making the call.

GREEN LIGHT
FUNDRAISING

5. Identifying who will ask for the commitment.

   Identify who at the meeting will ask the person to commit to being chairperson.

6. Approaching the candidate at the meeting.

   Begin the meeting with pleasantries and enjoying the meal together. At the right moment the person who invited the candidate will open the subject of asking the person to be the chairperson. If the person who opens the subject is not comfortable in explaining the need for the campaign, she can defer to the executive director.

7. Describing the campaign and the commitment being requested.

   The executive director should describe the purpose of the campaign, the goal, a few sentences of background on the organization, a brief summary of the role of the campaign chairperson, and the estimated time commitment. The executive director should also tell a brief, captivating story of a life transformed by the work of the nonprofit. Invite questions from the candidate.

8. Each person speaks.

   Each person at the meeting should speak, affirming that the candidate is the right person for the job.

   Keep in mind Cialdini's principle of consensus: People will be likely to say yes to your request if you give them evidence that people just like them have been saying yes to it. You may be able to have the person there who has volunteered to head up asking each board member to give. If so, that person should mention the role to which they've committed.. Other persons at the meeting may offer to volunteer for the campaign.

9. The development director.

   The development director is there because she is the primary liaison between the organization and the campaign. Either she or the executive director can assure the candidate that the campaign will be highly organized, making it possible for the campaign chair to carry out her duties without worrying about the details.

Need More Help From Rich? See p. 241

GREEN LIGHT
FUNDRAISING

10. Asking for the commitment.

Once everyone has had a chance to speak, and the candidate's questions have been answered, the agreed upon person asks if the candidate will take the position. Then, it is time for silence, giving the candidate a chance to think and respond.

11. Yes!

If the person says yes, thank him or her. Then the executive director or the development director will say that they'll be in touch to set up the first meeting to go over the next tasks that need be accomplished in the campaign— recruiting the other campaign leaders and obtaining the lead gift.

12. No.

If the person says no, thank them for their time. If possible, leave the door open for the person to serve as campaign chair at a later date. Also, ask if they know anyone whom they would like to recommend to the pre-campaign committee for the chairperson post.

13. Maybe.

The person may say they need to consult with their spouse or think about it. If that's the case, ask the person when they will have an answer, and the executive director should commit to calling the person on that date.

If you've followed these steps and you have your campaign chairperson, celebrate. If you followed these steps and the answer was no, you will have learned from the experience and be even more comfortable in the recruitment meeting of the person next on the list.

You will find a checklist for the steps to successfully recruiting a campaign chairperson on the Green Light Fundraising website at http://greenlightfundraising.org/downloads/recruiting.doc.

GREEN LIGHT
FUNDRAISING

Leading by giving the lead gift

You now have your campaign chairperson and you are ready to seek the lead gift. It's called a lead gift because its size determines the success of the entire campaign. An Italian economist, Vilfredo Pareto, studied the distribution of wealth in Italy in the early 20th century. He discovered that 80% of the land was owned by 20% of the people. He noted a similar distribution of wealth.

Others followed up on his work and discovered that often a business received 80% of its profit from 20% of it customers. Eventually, fundraisers noticed that contributions to a campaign follow a similar pattern with 80% of the total amount raised coming from 20% of the donors. Fundraisers began to create gift charts based on the 80-20 rule to show donors the levels of gifts needed to successfully achieve the campaign goal.

Gift charts show the number of gifts needed at each level to meet the goal distributing the gifts across the chart so that 80% of the income comes from 20% of the donors.

Standard gift charts for capital campaigns set the lead gift at 10% of the goal, but, as I mentioned in Chapter 5, when I work with clients, I usually encourage them to set the lead gift at 15% of the total goal. Since they will be doing a campaign every year, it gives them an opportunity to grow the total amount raised each year for several years without increasing the size of the lead gift each year.

> As a nonprofit you have no influence over the capacity of a person to give but you can influence the motivation of a person to give.

Now that you have a campaign chairperson and you know the size of the lead gift, it's time to set up a meeting of the pre-campaign committee and the new campaign chairperson. The meeting will have three purposes. First, the pre-campaign committee can help the campaign chairperson to identify three to four candidates for each of the leadership positions. The responsibility for actually recruiting the other leadership positions has shifted to the campaign chairperson, because it works best for the chairperson to recruit people he knows and trusts to do a good job. Still, it will be helpful for the chairperson to have recommendations from the pre-campaign committee.

Need More Help From Rich? See p. 241

GREEN LIGHT
FUNDRAISING

The development director should brief the campaign chairperson and the pre-campaign committee on the responsibilities of each of the following leadership positions. You can find sample role descriptions for each of these positions on the Green Light Fundraising website:

- Advance gifts chairperson

  http://greenlightfundraising.org/downloads/advance.doc

- Special Gifts chairperson

  http://greenlightfundraising.org/downloads/special.doc

- Chairperson for geographic or other solicitation divisions of the campaign

  http://greenlightfundraising.org/downloads/division.doc

- Marketing chairperson

  http://greenlightfundraising.org/downloads/marketing.doc

While the campaign chairperson is the chief recruiter for these key positions, he or she may involve members of the pre-campaign committee in recruiting campaign leaders if they have a relationship with the candidates. Again, rank the three to four people for each position so that you have a sequence of people to ask if the recruiters are told no.

Identifying potential givers of the lead gift

There's a story that when Robert Schuller decided to build the Crystal Cathedral, he knew that he was going to have to raise more money than he ever had before. He called up a major donor to ask for advice. The donor asked, "How do you catch a moose?"

Schuller realized he needed to go where the moose are. He identified the top potential givers in the USA. I wasn't able to verify this story, but apparently Schuller obtained the lead gift for the Crystal Cathedral campaign from an individual who was part of another denomination. When his multi-million dollar gift became public, officials from his denomination asked the donor why he gave so much money to the Schuller campaign and not his own denomination. "You never asked," he said.

To identify four to five prospective candidates for the lead gift, encourage each member of the pre-campaign committee, prior to the meeting, to e-mail the development director one or two names of people they know who have the capacity to give the lead gift.

There is a difference between the capacity to give and the motivation to give. Capacity to give means the potential giver has sufficient wealth to make a one-time gift of the size of the lead gift. Motivation means the person believes in the organization and its ability to transform lives, and that he or she is likely to give to the campaign.

The first step is to identify community members with the capacity to give. Motivation will help you to rank the community members. When you ask the pre-campaign committee to identify people with the capacity to give the lead gift, be sure to explain the difference between capacity to give and the motivation to give and that, at this stage, we are considering capacity only. Remember, as a nonprofit you have no influence over the capacity of a person to give, but you can influence the motivation of a person to give.

Let's assume that the members of the pre-campaign committee have e-mailed you, the development director, the names of five different individuals who have the capacity to give the lead gift. Now it's time for you to do your homework to assist the pre-campaign committee in assessing the motivation of each of the potential lead gift givers. Use your organization's donor database to research each person on the list. Develop a brief report for each person:

- Identify the number of gifts the person has given to your nonprofit;
- Identify the largest gift given and the purpose of the gift;
- Identify who solicited the gift;
- Identify how long the person has been a donor;
- Identify if the person held any volunteer or staff roles within your nonprofit;
- Identify who on your nonprofit's staff has been the primary contact person;
- Contact the executive director to identify any business dealings that each prospect may have had with your nonprofit; and
- Any other pertinent information you have about the person.

GREEN LIGHT
FUNDRAISING

Hopefully, you will have identified a number of the potential lead givers who already have connections to your organization and are likely to be motivated to give. But, if your research doesn't show any connections, don't worry. Remember, your nonprofit has no influence over the capacity of a person to give, but you can influence the motivation of a person to give.

> When you complete your first campaign, you will realize that success is a combination of good planning, hard work and serendipity.

The $100,000 lead gift for the first capital campaign I directed came from a farmer who had no record in our donor file. He heard about the capital campaign and offered to give the lead gift even before we had gotten to the stage of soliciting a lead gift. Yes, sometimes these things happen. He was on the board of a bank that employed one of our board members. Her son had been helped much by the organization, a fact the she freely told people. One day, while the campaign was still in the planning stages, she told the gentleman about the proposed campaign and how it would help her son and many other people. Later he stopped by her desk and said that he would like to give the lead gift.

When you complete your first campaign, you will realize that success is a combination of good planning, hard work by a lot of people, and serendipity.

When the pre-campaign committee and the campaign chairperson get to the point in the meeting where they will rank the potential lead givers, you, as the development director, should present your report on each candidate's giving history and connection with the organization.

A person is motivated to give not only by their connections to the organization, but also connections with the people who ask for the gift. People at a certain level within a community are often accustomed to supporting each others' charitable causes.

The development director should make explicit that all conversations about a person's potential to give to the campaign need to be handled with complete confidentiality. Nothing is more likely to tarnish your campaign and organization than for someone to share the confidential information outside the meeting.

GREEN LIGHT
FUNDRAISING

The campaign chairperson and the pre-campaign committee should go through each name and share any additional information that will help determine the ranking of the order in which the prospects will be approached and asked for the lead gift. Such information may include:

- Business deals in the works that may influence the person's ability to give;

- Business and personal relationships with the campaign chairperson and others on the pre-campaign committee that may influence who should ask for the gift;

- Any personal or family connections the person may have with someone who has been served by the nonprofit;

- Any personal or family connections with board members or staff, past and present; and

- Other pertinent information.

Once the group has identified all of the pertinent information on each person, the group should then rank them according to the order in which they will be approached and asked for the lead gift.

Once the ranking is completed, develop a plan for asking the first person on the list.

The role of the development director is to coach the campaign chairperson, pre-campaign committee and executive director in taking steps to secure the lead gift. It's a task that calls for maximum diplomacy. The director of development will have to be sensitive to how well-versed and experienced the group is in securing major gifts and fill in only information on the steps when it is needed.

The first step in the process of securing the lead gift is to identify who will be part of meeting with the potential lead giver. While the number of people who meet with the person may vary, depending on the circumstances, I recommend two to three people:

- The executive director, who can provide an overview of the work of the nonprofit and the need for the campaign. And he or she is in the position of telling a story of a life transformed by the work of the nonprofit.

- The campaign chairperson, who can explain how important the lead gift is, since it sets the pace for the rest of the campaign. Also, he or she can explain that someone else will be invited to provide the lead gift next year making the lead gift request a one-time request.

GREEN LIGHT
FUNDRAISING

- If someone on the pre-campaign committee or board has a closer relationship with the prospect, he or she can be included in the group meeting with the prospect.

Once you have determined who will be part of the conversation with the top lead gift prospect, you can use the same steps I outlined in recruiting the campaign chairperson above.

You have now completed the steps to successfully obtain the lead gift. If the group was successful, celebrate.

If the group was not successful, you already have a back-up plan because the lead gift prospects were ranked. The rule of thumb in face-to-face fundraising: You need three to four prospects for every gift you need to be successful. Your organization may need to approach three to four people to obtain the lead gift.

It's time to move on to the second person on your list. Repeat the steps.

You will find a checklist for successfully obtaining the lead gift on the Green Light Fundraising website at http://greenlightfundraising.org/downloads/lead.doc.

The secret to persistence

You are sure to have times of disappointment in each campaign. I had many setbacks in the first campaign that I directed—the campaign to move adults with developmental disabilities from a nursing home to small group homes. Through that campaign, I discovered the secret of motivating myself to persist in a campaign.

When the going got tough during the campaign, I would think about Gene, the president of the resident council. When the topic of moving to a small group home came up, Gene would say, "You know me, I like peace and quiet." As long as he lived in that nursing home he was not going to have peace and quiet.

When I would picture Gene, I would think, "I would do anything to help him live in a place where he could have his peace and quiet." And then I would put the setback behind me and I would push on with the next phone call, the next conversation, or the next campaign report that was going to take us one step closer to getting Gene the peace and quiet for which he longed.

GREEN LIGHT
FUNDRAISING

The secret to persisting in recruiting campaign leaders and overcoming the challenges that arise in any campaign is to have a clear picture in your mind of someone whose life will be transformed by the funds that you raise.

Looking ahead

You are now ready to move full speed ahead with learning to recruit the rest of the volunteers. In the next chapter we'll tell you the secrets of putting together a winning team.

How can we improve?

E-mail us at (comment@greenlightfundraising.org) to let us know when something is unclear, or you have a suggestion for improving the book. Please identify the page and paragraph that needs improving.

CHAPTER 12

Recruiting: The Best Team Wins

Some older boys taught my son how to dribble a basketball before he was age two. Thus began his love affair with basketball. One night at dinner, when he was eight, Jon stood up after dinner and announced that he hadn't played basketball yet that day so he was going out to play. He told us that he has to play every day. "It's a commitment," he said.

That commitment, plus natural talent, and the fact that he grew to be 6'8" meant that the summer between his junior and senior years of high school he began to be recruited by college basketball programs. Gradually, I realized that colleges are very systematic in their recruiting. They gather as much information as possible on potential recruits—strengths and weaknesses as a player compared to the needs of their team, the potential of the player for improvement, and the player's academic abilities. They also research the family because they want to know who in the family is going to have the most influence on the player's college decision. In fact, there are companies that specialize in evaluating players and selling the information to colleges.

Eventually Jon signed with Colgate University in upstate New York.

What impressed me about Colgate is that they not only did a good job of recruiting Jon, but as soon as he registered with them, they sent Sarah and me a recruiting letter, giving us various options for helping the University with their fundraising. Grateful that they had given my son the opportunity to play the game he loved at a Division 1 level, I signed up to call five other Colgate parents to ask them to donate to the University's Family Fund that year.

Division 1 basketball programs in the USA spend a lot of money on recruiting because they know that, no matter how good the school is and no matter how good the coach is, unless they have the best players, they don't win.

Likewise, as a nonprofit no matter how great your cause is, you'll have difficulty with your sustainable fundraising unless you recruit a great team of volunteers.

GREEN LIGHT FUNDRAISING

How many volunteers do you need?

Just like basketball coaches evaluate their team to determine the type of players they need to recruit, you need to evaluate the number of volunteers you need to run a successful campaign. Thankfully, by following three simple rules, you can use your gift chart to determine precisely the number of volunteers you need.

For every gift, you need three prospects.

For every five prospects, you need one volunteer solicitor.

For every five volunteer solicitors, you need one team captain.

> By following three rules, you can use your gift chart to determine precisely the number of volunteers you need.

Let's use the sample gift chart from Chapter 5 to determine the number of prospects and volunteers needed:

Gift Chart for $100,000

Segment	# of gifts	Size of gift	Total	Prospects	total by phase	# of solicitors
Lead	1	$ 15,000.00	$ 15,000.00	3		
Advance	1	$ 10,000.00	$ 10,000.00	3		
Advance	2	$ 7,500.00	$ 15,000.00	6		
Advance	3	$ 5,000.00	$ 15,000.00	9		
Advance	6	$ 2,500.00	$ 15,000.00	18		
Advance	7	$ 1,500.00	$ 10,500.00	21	57	11.4
Special	8	$ 1,000.00	$ 8,000.00	24		
Special	9	$ 500.00	$ 4,500.00	27		
Special	10	$ 250.00	$ 2,500.00	30		
Special	15	$ 100.00	$ 1,500.00	45	126	25.2
Under $100	Varies	$ 3,000.00	$ 3,000.00			
TOTAL			$ 100,000.00			
				Lead gift & advance gifts		80%
			80/20 rule	$ 80,500.00		$ 80,000.00
# of advance gift captains needed			2.28	2		
# of special gift captains needed			5.04	5		

The chart reveals that we need 57 advance prospects that have the capacity to give between $1,500 and $10,000. In order to have a solicitor for each of the five prospects, we need eleven solicitors and two captains.

The chart reveals that we need 126 special gifts prospects that have the capacity to give between $100 and $1,000. In order to have a solicitor for each of the five prospects, we need 25 solicitors and five captains.

The circumstances will vary from nonprofit to nonprofit. In the example above, it assumes a special event or mailing will bring in $3,000 in gifts under $100. However, if you already have an event or appeal that can bring in $10,000, you can include that in the gift chart and have the minimum gift asked for face-to-face be $250. Then your chart might look like the following:

Gift Chart for $100,000

Segment	# of gifts	Size of gift	Total	Prospects	total by phase	# of solici-tors
Lead	1	$ 15,000.00	$ 15,000.00	3		
Advance	1	$ 10,000.00	$ 10,000.00	3		
Advance	2	$ 7,500.00	$ 15,000.00	6		
Advance	3	$ 5,000.00	$ 15,000.00	9		
Advance	4	$ 2,500.00	$ 10,000.00	12		
Advance	5	$ 1,500.00	$ 7,500.00	15	48	9.6
Special	8	$ 1,000.00	$ 8,000.00	24		
Special	10	$ 500.00	$ 5,000.00	30		
Special	18	$ 250.00	$ 4,500.00	54	108	21.6
Year-end appeal		$ 10,000.00	$ 10,000.00			25.2
TOTAL			$100,000.00			
				Lead gift & advance gifts		80%
			80/20 rule	$72,500.00		$ 80,000.00
# of advance gift captains needed			1.92	2		
# of special gift captains needed			4.32	8		

Need More Help From Rich? See p. 241

GREEN LIGHT
FUNDRAISING

I show you two different charts in order to give you an example of how you can adapt the gift chart to the particular circumstances of your nonprofit. In the second chart, we reduced the lead and advance gifts total to $72,500, under the assumption that the number of givers will increase substantially due to the $10,000 appeal or special event so that $72,500 will still keep the 80/20 rule, with $72,500 being the amount give by 20% of the donors. The result was that we reduced the number of prospects needed for advance gifts from 57 prospects to 48, the number of advance gifts solicitors needed from 11 to 10. As you can see that's a significant reduction in the number of volunteers you need at the advance gifts level. In the second chart, the number of special gifts prospects is reduced from 126 to 108, decreasing the need for solicitors by one from 25 to 21. The number of special gifts captains decrease by one.

You can find the Excel spreadsheets used to create the two sample gift charts above as a free download at http://greenlightfundraising.org/downloads/giftchart1.xls and http://greenlightfundraising.org/downloads/giftchart2.xls.

Once you've created a gift chart for your campaign, complete with the number of prospects needed, solicitors, and captains you need, you are ready to create your recruiting plan.

Who does the recruiting?

Successful recruiting is based on a simple principle:

Volunteer leaders recruit their own teams.

There are three important advantages to volunteer leaders recruiting their own teams. First, your nonprofit wants its volunteer leaders and their teams to succeed. When you allow volunteer leaders to choose their own teams, you increase their chances of success. Volunteer leaders don't have the controls of traditional tools of employment. Their success depends on their ability to lead through relationships and they increase their likelihood of success by being able to choose people with whom they already have relationships. The first tool you give your volunteer leaders is the ability to choose their own teams.

Second, in order to succeed, volunteer leaders need results from their solicitors. They need each volunteer on their team to set up face-to-face meetings with potential givers, ask for, and receive gifts; i.e. they need their volunteers to be accountable for results. Without the formal authority of an employment relationship, it's much easier for volunteer leaders to get positive results from friends they have personally selected for the task.

Third, inevitably volunteer leaders will have to give a gentle nudge to a team member or two to get positive results. A captain may not have completed recruiting her team yet, and the deadline is approaching. It's time for a gentle nudge. A solicitor may have made his calls, but not followed up yet to get a yes or no, and the deadline is approaching. In each case, it's time for a gentle nudge. When you know someone well, you are more likely to know a good way to give that gentle nudge without offending the person.

Start at the top

In Chapter 11 we covered recruiting the campaign chairperson. Now it's time to recruit the advance gifts and special gifts chairperson. Let's start with the advance gifts chairperson.

Advance gifts - the quiet phase - chairperson and captains

Recruiting the advance gifts chairperson is a top priority of the campaign chairperson. The campaign chairperson will likely team up with the executive director in advance gifts recruiting meetings since the

> Timely recruiting is essential for a successful campaign.

executive director will be able to answer questions about the organization and the campaign and highlight the importance of the campaign to the potential recruit. Encourage the campaign chairperson to create a list of three to four potential advance gifts chairpersons, and rank them according to the best candidate first and so on. Then the campaign chairperson will have a recruiting plan.

For the advance gifts chairperson, you want someone who is well-respected and well-networked among upper-income people in the community. In fact, your advance gifts chairperson may also be the co-chairperson of the campaign in line to become next year's chairperson. You want the kind of person who is comfortable with recruiting

GREEN LIGHT FUNDRAISING

others to your cause, since his or her key role is to recruit the captains who in turn will recruit the advance gifts solicitors. You also need someone who will be assertive with a captain if one of the captain's team members is lagging in meeting with the potential givers he or she has committed to solicit.

You also want someone for whom others like to do things, since the advance gifts phase produces the most income in the campaign. The advance gifts phase is designed to bring in 65% to 70% of the overall financial goal. The lead gift, plus the advance gifts phase, should bring in 80% of the campaign goal in keeping with the 80-20 rule.

You can find a sample of role description for the advance gifts chairperson as a free download o the Green Light Fundraising website at http://greenlightfundraising.org/downloads/advance.doc

Assuming that your campaign goal is $100,000 using the first gift chart above, the advance gifts phase should raise gifts in the following ranges:

1 gift @ $10,000   3 gifts @ $5,000   7 gifts @ $1,500

2 gifts @ $7,500   6 gifts @ $ 2,500

In the scenario above, the advance gifts chairperson will recruit two captains who in turn, will each recruit five advance gifts solicitors. If at all possible, the advance gifts chairperson should be someone who has the capacity and willingness to donate at the advance gifts level, as should be the vice-chairpersons and solicitors.

Case statement as a recruiting tool

Use the case statement as a recruiting tool. If the case statement is not in its final form, when the advance gifts recruiting phase begins, use the current draft as a tool for recruiting.

Recruits want to know the answers to three questions:

1. Why should I volunteer for this nonprofit; i.e., how does the nonprofit transform lives?

2. The volunteer wants a simple answer to this question. Provide volunteer with the current draft of the case statement that provides great information on the work of the nonprofit. Point to a story in the case statement about a life transformed by the nonprofit.

3. What will be expected of me?

4. The volunteer will be expected to attend a kickoff/training session and ask five people to make a gift in the range of (insert advance gifts range). The case statement contains the gift range, which will be helpful in describing the role of the advance gifts volunteer in the context of the entire campaign.

5. What will be my time commitment?

6. Give the volunteer the date of kickoff, advance gifts solicitation phase time period (usually four weeks), and the date of the celebration of the campaign's success. The volunteer is committing enough time to attend the kickoff, make appointments and meet with five people to request a gift, and to attend the celebration.

The timeline as a recruiting tool

The timeline will be your guide as to when you need to have the advance gifts chairperson recruited. It will also help you to provide a deadline for the advance gifts chairperson to recruit her captains. In turn, the timeline also lets the captains know their deadline for recruiting the advance gifts solicitors.

Using a recruiting scorecard to celebrate recruiting

Timely recruiting is essential for a successful campaign. One mechanism for encouraging timely recruiting is to use a scorecard that you update for each weekly e-mail during the recruiting period. At a glance, the scorecard highlights each week's success on the recruiting front. Here's a sample of a completed advanced gifts scorecard, based on the Gift Chart 2 above, assuming that you have two captains who need to recruit five solicitors each:

Need More Help From Rich? See p. 241

GREEN LIGHT
FUNDRAISING

Advance Gifts Solicitor Recruits Scorecard						
Captain	Goal	Week 1	Week 2	Week 3	Week 4	Success!
John Deere	5	1	3	0	1	5
Alice Chalmers	5	2	2	1		5
Total	10	3	5	1	1	10

In the example above, in your e-letter at the end of Week 1, your score care would look like this:

Advance Gifts Solicitor Recruits Scorecard						
Captain	Goal	Week 1	Week 2	Week 3	Week 4	Success!
John Deere	5	1				1
Alice Chalmers	5	2				2
Total	10	3				3

At a glance, you can tell that after one week John has recruited one solicitor and Alice has recruited two for a total of three out of the ten needed.

As soon as someone is recruited you should celebrate the success in the e-letter update and provide a two to three sentence bio of the person who was recruited. That means you, as the development director, will need to be in ouch regularly with the advance gifts chairperson and the captains so that you can report progress on recruiting.

Building campaign momentum through the quiet phase

The advance gifts phase of a campaign is often referred to as the quiet phase of the campaign. For a campaign to be successful, you want to build momentum. The first stage of building momentum begins with the lead gift. Securing the lead gift builds tremendous momentum. The second stage of building momentum is the advance gifts stage. It's called the quiet phase because it happens before the media blitz that is essential to help the special gifts phase to put you over the top. You want to have raised 60% to 80% of your goal before you go public with the launch of the special gifts phase. That builds tremendous momentum for the campaign.

The concept of the quiet phase can become a selling point during the advance gifts phase. Solicitors can be upfront with potential advance gifts donors that they are part of a small group of people who are being asked to make larger gifts early in the campaign to build momentum for a successful campaign.

Remember the six universal principles of influence that we covered in chapter 11? The principle of scarcity can be applied here: "People will try to seize the opportunities that you offer them that are rare or dwindling in availability." Solicitors are offering advance gifts prospects the rare opportunity be one of the few people who make a gift that will dramatically build momentum for the campaign and will lead others to give as well.

Earlier I mentioned that the advance gifts chairperson should give at the advance gifts level. The same is true of each of the advance gifts captains and team members. The reason that the advance gifts team should give first is an application of consensus, one of the six universal principles of influence that we covered in chapter 11 "People will be likely to say yes to your request if you give them evidence that people just like them have been saying yes to it."

Recently Evergreen Leaders did a campaign to underwrite the cost of writing and designing this ebook. The chairperson of the campaign pledged but then when he saw the gift chart he upped his gift to the advance gifts range because he wanted to be able to say to potential donors that he met with that he had given at the advance gifts level.

 Need More Help From Rich? See p. 241
GREEN LIGHT FUNDRAISING

Special gifts – recruiting the chairperson and captains

Recruiting the special gifts chairperson is the second priority of the campaign chairperson after the advance gifts chairperson. The campaign chairperson will likely team up with the executive director in special gifts recruiting meetings, since the executive director will be able to answer questions regarding the organization and the campaign and highlight the importance of the campaign with regard to the organization's mission. Encourage the campaign chairperson to create a list of three to four potential special gifts chairpersons, and rank them according to the best candidate first and so on. Then the campaign chairperson will have a recruiting plan.

Special gifts chairperson is often a good position for a younger, up-and-coming leader in your community. Like the advance gifts chair, you want someone who is well-respected and well-networked amoin the community. You want the kind of person who is comfortable with recruiting others to your cause, since their key role is to recruit the captains who, in turn, will recruit the special gifts solicitors. You also need someone who will be assertive with a captain if one of the captains' team members is lagging in meeting with the potential givers whom she has committed to solicit.

You need someone who is people and goal-oriented. Cialdini's principle on liking applies here: "People prefer to say yes to your request to the degree that they know and like you. No surprise there." Look for a young leader in the community who is well-liked. You can find a model role description for the special gifts chairperson at the Green Light Fundraising website at http://greenlightfundraising.org/downloads/special.doc

The special gifts phase of a campaign is designed to put the campaign over the top. The better the special gifts team does, the more you go over your goal.

Assuming that your campaign goal is $100,000, using the first gift chart above, the special gifts phase should raise gifts in the following ranges:

8 gifts @ $1000   9 gifts @ $500   10 gifts @ $250   15 gifts @ $100

In the scenario above, the special gifts chairperson will recruit four captains who in turn will each recruit five special gifts solicitors. If at all possible, the special gifts chairperson should be someone who has the capacity and willingness to donate at

GREEN LIGHT
FUNDRAISING

the mid to upper range of the special gifts. The captains and solicitors should give generously in the special gifts range, depending on their capacity.

The timeline is your guide for setting the deadlines for recruiting the special gifts chairperson, special gifts captains, and the special gifts solicitors.

Timely recruiting is essential for a successful campaign. Like we suggested in the section for the advance gifts chairperson, using a scorecard in weekly campaign e-mail updates during the recruiting period encourages your recruiters.

At a glance, the scorecard highlights each week's success on the recruiting front. Here's a sample of a completed special gifts scorecard, based on Gift Chart 2 above, assuming you have four captains who need to recruit five solicitors each:

Special Gifts Solicitor Recruits Scorecard						
Captain	Goal	Week 1	Week 2	Week 3	Week 4	Success!
Jan Ford	6	1	3	0	2	6
Bill Chevy	6	2	2	1	1	6
Tammy Toyota	5	0	0	1	4	5
Helen Honda	5	1	4			5
James Bentley	5	5				5
Total	27	9	9	2	7	27

 Need More Help From Rich? See p. 241
GREEN LIGHT
FUNDRAISING

In the example above in your e-letter at the end of Week 3 your score care would look like this:

Special Gifts Solicitor Recruits Scorecard						
Captain	Goal	Week 1	Week 2	Week 3	Week 4	Success!
Jan Ford	5	1	3	0		4
Bill Chevy	5	2	2	1		5
Tammy Toyota	5	0	0	1		1
Helen Honda	5	1	4			5
James Bentley	5	5				5
Total	25	9	9	2		20

The above scorecard shows that Jan needs one more recruit to meet her goal. The scorecard also shows that you need to be concerned about Tammy. In the first three weeks she has only recruited one of her goal of five. The special gifts chairperson needs to check with her to see how likely it is that she will reach her goal in the next week. She may well still make her goal but you need to know because, if she's not going to, the special gifts chairperson may need to recruit a replacement or serve as a captain also to make up for the hole that Tammy's lack of recruiting will cause in the campaign. Hopefully, she's one who waits until the last minute to meet a deadline, but the only way you'll know is if her chairperson talks to her. In fact, her chairperson should have been talking to her each week of the recruiting period for her report.

I use the example of Tammy making only one recruit in the first three weeks of the recruiting period to highlight a reality of the campaign. Expect the unexpected, and be ready to create a backup plan. You may discover that Tammy's husband has suddenly taken ill and she will not be able to serve as a team captain.

Use weekly e-mail updates to highlight each week's success on the recruiting front. In addition to the report card, list the names of each new recruit, and include a two-sentence bio for to create a sense of belonging and commitment to the campaign.

GREEN LIGHT
FUNDRAISING

Recruiting orientations

Once you have recruited your advance gifts and special gifts chairpersons, your campaign will move into the recruiting phase of the campaign. Remember, the best team wins and you obtain the best team through great recruiting. Recruiting captains and solicitors for the campaign is such an essential part of making your campaign a success that I recommend that you develop a brief recruiting orientation. First, orient the advance gifts and special gifts chairpersons to the best way to recruit their team captains. The ideal is to orient the advance and special gifts chairpersons at the same time to ensure than they are not recruiting the same people as captains. If you orient them separately, have the advance gifts chairperson select the captains he will recruit first and then give his list to the special gifts chairperson to make sure they are not recruiting the same people.

Orienting chairpersons to recruiting team captains

Your recruiting orientation for advance and special gifts chairpersons should include the following elements:

1. Enthusiasm for the cause.

   Create enthusiasm for the cause through a story of how your nonprofit transforms lives and through a brief outline of how the campaign will help your nonprofit to transform lives. If possible, have the executive director tell the story.

2. Paint a picture of a great recruit. An ideal recruit for a captain is:

   - Community-minded;

   - Well-respected and well-liked;

   - Able to give generously within the range of the phase in which they are working;

   - Has a network of friends from whom he can recruit five excellent solicitors;

   - Knows the best team wins; and

   - Has a reputation for following through

Need More Help From Rich? See p. 241

GREEN LIGHT
FUNDRAISING

3. Each chairperson develops a recruiting list.

Prior to the recruiting orientation, have each chairperson e-mail you a list of ten people they can potentially recruit. The assignment will prime the pump on their recruiting since it's always easier to recruit from a list of potential recruits. Make copies for each captain of all the lists. At the orientation meetings the captains can compare lists and eliminate duplicates by agreeing who will approach any duplicate names.

4. Go over the recruiting timeline for recruiting captains.

Your campaign timeline includes a recruiting period for the advance gifts solicitors and special gifts solicitors. I recommend doing the recruiting over no more than a four-week period for each of the recruiting periods.

5. Go over the scorecard and the weekly report days.

Give each captain a scorecard that lists the captains and each of their goals. Ask them to e-mail their chairperson and cc you on each week's report day, indicating the number of yeses they have received. Let them know that a day later, they will receive an e-mail update with that week's updated scorecard. Tell them that you'd like to include a two sentence bio of each recruit in the update and they can either include it in their e-mail report or you'll call them and they can give the bios to you over the phone.

> Remember, the best team wins and you obtain the best team through great recruits.

Planning and executing the solicitor recruiting orientation meetings

Plan each solicitor recruiting orientation meeting with the appropriate chairperson and the executive director. The executive director is the best person to create enthusiasm for the cause and, if at all possible, should take that role. The chairperson and the development director can divide up the other items in the orientation.

Give each captain a scorecard, several copies of the case statement for use in recruiting, and a handout called "Ten tips for recruiting a great team."

GREEN LIGHT
FUNDRAISING

Ten tips for recruiting a great team

1. Recruit people you know.

   You've already done things for people you know and they are more likely to say yes to you.

2. Tell them the benefits.

   Think through the possible benefits for them. Will it build their network? Will it build goodwill for their company? Will it add to their resume? When you ask, be ready to tell them how it will benefit them.

3. Tell them why you volunteered.

   Stories are the best way to describe a cause and telling your own story as to why you are volunteering for the campaign is an effective way of communicating the value of the cause.

4. Tell them what to expect.

   Tell potential recruits exactly what will be expected of them:

   - How many meetings they will be expected to attend
   - The range of gift they will be expected to give
   - How many people they will be expected to meet in person to ask for a gift
   - The range of gifts that they will be asking for.

5. Tell them why you are asking them.

   People like to hear good things about themselves and you have good reasons for asking this person. Tell them.

6. Tell them who is already on board.

   One of Cialdini's principles of influence I've covered earlier applies here: "People will be likely to say yes to your request if you give them evidence that people just like them have been saying yes to it." Consider telling them who the campaign chairperson is, who the advance gifts and special gifts chairpersons are, and anyone else that you have recruited.

Need More Help From Rich? See p. 241

GREEN LIGHT
FUNDRAISING

7. Listen to hesitations.

People who you are recruiting are likely to have hesitations. Listen respectfully to any hesitations. Suggest ways of dealing with the hesitations that will be good for them and good for the campaign.

8. Give them time to think about it.

Most people you recruit will want a little time to think about it. Ask them when would be a good time to call them back for their answer.

9. Respect a no.

Not everyone will be able to volunteer. Be respectful when people tell you no. If you've used these tips, you've done your job well, even when you are told no. Also, when someone has said no to one request, they are more likely to say yes to another. The person who says no to volunteering may say yes to giving a generous gift.

10. Be grateful.

Thank them for giving you the time to talk with them about the project. Thank them for considering. When they say yes, be grateful again and send them a note of thanks.

You can find "Ten tips to recruiting a great team" as a free download on the Green Light Fundraising at http://greenlightfundraising.org/downloads/tentips.pdf.

Follow the steps in this chapter and you'll give your volunteer leaders the tools to recruit a great team. Remember that great recruits lead to great teams who raise an amazing amount of money to help your nonprofit transform lives.

Looking ahead

Now you are ready to learn how the inner circle of your organization—board, staff, alumni, and families—plays a leadership role in the campaign.

How can we improve?

E-mail us at (comment@greenlightfundraising.org) to let us know when something is unclear, or you have a suggestion for improving the book. Please identify the page and paragraph that needs improving.

GREEN LIGHT
FUNDRAISING

CHAPTER 13

The Inner Circle: Priming The Pump

"Finding the center of strength within ourselves is in the long run the best contribution we can make to our fellow men. ... One person with indigenous inner strength exercises a great calming effect on panic among people around him. This is what our society needs — not new ideas and inventions; important as these are, and not geniuses and supermen, but persons who can "be", that is, persons who have a center of strength within themselves."

— Rollo May (Man's Search for Himself)

Recently we had a fire at the rural religious community to which I belong. A duplex burned. Thankfully, everyone in the family who was living there at the time made it outside safely and no one was seriously injured. Still, many people in our community witnessed the speed with which fire can envelop a building. The family living there lost almost everything and the building was a complete loss.

People in my community were traumatized. For the next week, I spent a lot of time listening to people. Since the fire investigators could not determine the cause, rumors spread as people tried to fit the pieces of the puzzle together. I listened, dealt with the press, and stayed calm. I've been a member of this community for over thirty years and, thus, I've see the community go through a lot of ups and downs. I have a basic trust that together we'll be able to handle whatever life throws at us. With a little help from above, I was able to listen, stay calm, and see others begin to calm down too.

Just like one person with a calm center can have a calming effect on a group of people, the people at the center of your organization—the board, staff, those served and their families—can have an energizing and encouraging effect on the entire campaign.

When you ask for gifts from the community, it's natural for donors to wonder if the people closest to the need are also giving. The inner circle is designed to answer that question with a resounding yes.

I call the giving by the inner circle "priming the pump." When I was a youngster living on a farm in northern Minnesota, we had a hand water pump. Occasionally we would pump the handle up and down and no water would come out. It was time to prime the pump. We'd pour water into the pump and then pump and, soon, water would begin flowing out of the pump.

GREEN LIGHT
FUNDRAISING

The giving by the inner circle has the same effect. When the board and staff have given to the campaign, potential donors know that the campaign is important and that gifts will flow like water from a primed pump.

Now don't worry if most of your board members do not consider themselves to be fundraisers. Many community nonprofits have boards that are made up of people who have a passion for the cause of the nonprofit but are frightened of fundraising.

By now you will have noticed that the Green Light Fundraising model does not depend on a board of directors who loves asking for money. The board is expected to help with recruiting the campaign leadership but the bulk of the asking for funds is done by volunteers who are not on the board.

Creating a campaign committee separate from the board is by design. I have long ago given up trying to persuade people to do something they don't want to do. It's a waste of time. Fundraising is not sustainable if it depends on people who would rather have a tooth pulled without anesthesia than ask someone for a gift.

If Green Light Fundraising depended on persuading a recalcitrant board suddenly to go out and ask lots of people for money, it would fail before it started.

Yet the board does play three important roles in the campaign: first, they approve the campaign; second, they give to the campaign; and third, they are ambassadors for the campaign in their circles of influence.

Usually, major initiatives, such as launching sustainable fundraising are approved by the board. There are four good reasons to seek the approval of the board.

First, you want to outline the campaign in a proposal to the board because you want it tested by the leaders of your community on your board. If your board members, who know your community, have suggestions on how to improve the plan, it will be stronger.

Need More Help From Rich? See p. 241

GREEN LIGHT
FUNDRAISING

Second, you want buy-in from the board, because they are the frontline ambassadors of your nonprofit to friends and colleagues about the campaign. As word of the campaign spreads through the community, people who know your board members will ask them about the campaign. If they've tested the campaign through a proposal to the board, they will be stronger ambassadors.

Third, the proposal is a good place to describe the role of the board in the campaign, including the fact that 100% of the board are expected to give.

Fourth, if the executive director and development director can successfully market the campaign to the board, they are likely to be able to market it to the community.

100% of the Board Gives

Giving to the campaign begins with the inner circle, those who are closest to the need. While not every board member will be asking for gifts, we expect 100% of the board members to give to the campaign.

The giving capacity will vary from board member to board member. We expect each board member to give generously according to their ability.

The rationale for 100% giving by the board is that they know the need best and, if they give 100%, it gives a powerful message to the volunteers, potential donors, and donors that giving to the campaign in important.

The ideal is the giving of the board and the campaign chairperson to total 10% to 15% of the campaign goal.

Organizing the Board Inner Circle Giving

The board chairperson should appoint two board members as co-chairpersons of the inner circle board giving phase. The responsibility of the board inner circle co-chairs is to solicit the other board members. If the board chairperson is comfortable in asking, she may appoint herself as one of the two board solicitors.

Set a timeline for the work of the co-chairs of the board to complete their solicitation of the board. It's important to complete the board inner circle phase before the advance gifts phase can be completed. Then, the fact that 100% of the board has given is part of the orientation of the advance gifts phase.

Designing the staff inner circle

In addition to the board, the staff is part of the inner circle. Like the board, they are closest to the need, and their giving sends a large signal to the other donors that the campaign is essential.

Organizing the staff inner circle campaign can be more complex than organizing the board inner circle phase, especially if your nonprofit hires people at relatively low wages.

For instance, the first sustainable fundraising campaign that I consulted with served adults with developmental disabilities and had many direct care staff members who earned a couple of dollars an hour above minimum wage.

Our challenge was to create a staff inner circle phase that staff would donate to willingly. In discussions with staff, we discovered that the incredibly caring direct care staff members often spent their own money on small items needed by the people they served.

The nonprofit also had a small foundation that gave grants to people with disabilities. With these two key pieces of information, we created a fund aimed directly at making it possible for direct care staff to make small purchases to meet the needs of the people they served. To minimize bureaucracy, staff members simply needed the approval of a team of a couple of managers to use the fund. Also, each time the fund was used, the amount and purpose of the use was published to all staff so that everyone on staff saw how their gifts were used.

The foundation agreed to match every gift the staff made to the fund, up to $5000 each year.

We called the fund the "We Match You Fund," based on the fact that the foundation was matching the gifts of staff members. We created a brochure that outlined the fund and how it could be used, and then invited staff to participate.

Need More Help From Rich? See p. 241

GREEN LIGHT
FUNDRAISING

We also recruited a well-liked staff person to be the chairperson and to recruit other staff members who met with staff members in their departments to explain the campaign, the role the staff inner circle played in the campaign, and how the "We Match You Fund" worked, and to invite staff members to give to the fund. We also worked with the accounting department to make it possible for staff to give through payroll deduction.

Giving to the "We Match You Fund" as part of the staff inner circle phase of the campaign has become popular in the seven years since they launched their first sustainable fundraising campaign. Staff members get to see their gifts at work throughout the year.

A staff-led special event

The direct service staff members of community nonprofits tend not to be well paid, and making a contribution to a campaign can be challenging. Some of my nonprofit clients have creative ways to participate in Green Light Fundraising.

The direct service staff of one other client decided to run an auction as their way of contributing as an inner circle. Staff members volunteered to gather auction items in the community and were active in the auction.

A direct service employee of another nonprofit loved making chocolates. She spent hours making chocolates and then sold them to fellow staff members as a way increase the number of staff participating in the inner circle.

The development staff should work with direct service staff to develop a plan for participation in the staff inner circle, giving in a way that works for the direct service staff members.

The staff inner circle score card

Like the board, the primary goal of the staff inner circle is 100 percent participation. With larger nonprofits, especially with those employing people at lower wages, this might be difficult.

I encourage you to create a score card that tracks the percentage of staff who participate. The score card does two things.

GREEN LIGHT
FUNDRAISING

As you can tell by now, (since I've repeated it often enough) I have a favorite principle when it comes to fundraising: "People will be likely to say yes to your request if you give them evidence that people just like them have been saying yes to it.

Use the staff inner circle score card to give the staff evidence that other staff, people just like them, have been saying yes to giving to the campaign.

Second, the scorecard can help each year's chairperson set a goal of increasing the percentage of staff who give to the campaign. Or, if the giving is 100%, to maintain the 100% level.

Families and those served participate in the inner circle

In planning for your Green Light Fundraising campaign, you should consider whether the current people who benefit from your nonprofit services, alumni, or family members, have the interest and ability to give.

When I worked with Horizon House, a couple of parents of people served, organized a group of parents to phone other parents to ask for gifts.

Depending on the type of person served, you may also be able to plan creative ways for those served and alumni to participate in inner circle giving.

Looking ahead

The advance and special gifts phases of the campaign bring in the most funds. To help the volunteers do a great job of raising funds, they need to have good lists of prospects from which to choose. In the next chapter, you'll learn the secrets of finding people in your community who have a talent for giving.

How can we improve?

E-mail us at (comment@greenlightfundraising.org) to let us know when something is unclear, or you have a suggestion for improving the book. Please identify the page and paragraph that needs improving.

GREEN LIGHT
FUNDRAISING

CHAPTER 14

Finding Donors With A Talent For Giving

The Gallup Organization has a great definition for talent: A recurring pattern of thought, feeling, or behavior that can be productively used.

My parents were farmers with eighth grade educations, but they were also talent spotters. When I was in fifth grade, they began having me milk the cows in the mornings before school. Before then my older brothers did the milking. My parents said that they had my younger brother and me do the milking because my older brothers went to high school and had to get on the bus earlier. That never quite made sense to me, since milking started at 5:00 a.m. and they didn't have to get on the school bus until 7:10 and we got on the bus at 7:30.

Many years later, when I was teaching leadership to nonprofit managers, my parents happened to mention to me that I was always the easiest to get up in the morning. They only had to call me once. Their comment was an aha! moment for me. I've always been a morning person, someone who gets up in the morning and usually feels great. My parents put that recurring pattern of feeling great in the morning to productive use by waking me up at 5:00 a.m. to do the milking. Many kids—adults too—would hate getting up at 5:00 a.m. to do the milking. Not me. I still have great memories of waking up on winter mornings and walking through the snow to the barn in the subzero weather of northern Minnesota to milk the cows.

The success of your campaign depends on your being able to identify a pool of people with a talent for giving. To identify a pool of potential donors in your community, you need talent-spotters. This chapter will teach you how systematically to spot the potential donors who will make your campaign a success, and how to recruit talent-spotters to help you identify a pool of potential donors in your community.

> The long term goal of sustainable fundraising is to create a recurring pattern of generous giving to your nonprofit by a growing set of donors.

The long-term goal of sustainable fundraising is to create a recurring pattern of generous giving to your nonprofit by a growing set of donors.

Need More Help From Rich? See p. 241

GREEN LIGHT
FUNDRAISING

You may already know people who have a talent for giving to your nonprofit—your current donors. I served for fourteen years as the development director for a nonprofit that specialized in special event fundraising. They had a donor base of several thousand names, most of whom had given gifts of less than $100.

When we decided to do a $1.2 million capital campaign, the organization had a treasure in the names in the donor file. We already had the names of a lot of people who had a talent for giving to our organization. Unfortunately, because for years we had focused on special events and a Christmas mailing, even people with the capacity to give large gifts were used to giving small gifts. Still, we had lots of names, addresses and phone numbers on our donor management software of people who had given to us. Our management software was a great place to start finding donors with a talent for giving.

An aside about donor management software

You may have great donor management software that does all you want it to do and you are confident that it will meet all of the requirements of your sustainable fundraising campaign. Great. Skip this section and move on to building your prospect list.

But if you have a clunky donor management software, read on.

Your donor management software is the backbone of your ability to support the volunteers who will make your campaign a success. You need to be able to categorize your potential donors by the phase they will be solicited in. You need to be able to track which solicitor is soliciting which prospect. You need to be able to track which donors have been thanked, and whether it was by phone call, letter, or e-mail. You need to be able to handle pledges. You need to be able to handle winter and summer addresses.

You get the picture. To treat your volunteers and donors respectfully, you need to be highly organized, and good donor management software is a key to organizing a wide array of information on donors and prospects.

All too often nonprofits use Excel for their donor management software. Or, a volunteer may have built you a management software using Access. Or, a local computer guru may have talked you into having him build you fundraising management software that will fulfill your needs. That's the mistake I made.

GREEN LIGHT
FUNDRAISING

I started fundraising in the 1980's, when personal computers were first taking off. A local computer guru convinced me that he could create for us a great management software system for a flat fee. As I began using the management software I kept finding things it couldn't do and I'd ask him to ask him to add a feature. Soon, he said that he couldn't afford to add more features. Still, we had made a big investment, so we kept using it. Then we hired an assistant. In order to teach her how to use it independently of me, I wrote a 100+ page manual.

> Your donor management software is the backbone of your ability to support the volunteers who will make your campaign a success.

We limped along with the donor management software until I convinced our executive director that we needed to buy commercial fundraising management software with good telephone support and regular upgrades. Every year the company upgraded the software based on feedback from all their nonprofit customers. Not only that, but when my development assistant ran into a problem, I didn't need to be around to solve it. She simply called the company's tech support line. It was heavenly.

When I began consulting with other nonprofits who were using homemade donor management systems, I encouraged them to do the same thing. Buy commercial fundraising management software with good support and regular upgrades.

Recently, we did the research to secure donor management software for Evergreen Leaders. I not only wanted software that would serve our needs, but one that we could confidently recommend to clients. We settled on GiftWorks, an affordable, feature-rich system that has great online and phone support. For a free trial version of GiftWorks, click on http://greenlightfundraising.org/giftworks/. Full disclosure. Evergreen Leaders is a partner with GiftWorks and receives a modest fee for each GiftWorks sold through this link.

There are other good management software systems available also such as eTapestry, an online management software, and Raisers Edge from Blackbaud. The Nonprofit Technology Network regularly evaluates donor management software. Check them out at http://www.nten.org.

Need More Help From Rich? See p. 241

GREEN LIGHT
FUNDRAISING

If you have donor management software that is limping along, that can't produce all the reports you need, and that makes it cumbersome to track categories of prospects, this is a good time to upgrade your donor management software system. Remember, your donor management software is the backbone of your ability to support the volunteers who will make your campaign a success.

Building your prospect list

Your gift chart is the tool that helps you determine exactly the number of prospects you need for each giving phase of the campaign. The rule of thumb is that you need three prospects for every level of gift. Here's the sample gift chart that we used in chapter nine:

Gift Chart for $100,000

Segment	# of gifts	Size of gift	Total	Prospects	total by phase	# of solicitors
Lead	1	$ 15,000.00	$ 15,000.00	3		
Advance	1	$ 10,000.00	$ 10,000.00	3		
Advance	2	$ 7,500.00	$ 15,000.00	6		
Advance	3	$ 5,000.00	$ 15,000.00	9		
Advance	4	$ 2,500.00	$ 10,000.00	12		
Advance	5	$ 1,500.00	$ 7,500.00	15	48	9.6
Special	8	$ 1,000.00	$ 8,000.00	24		
Special	10	$ 500.00	$ 5,000.00	30		
Special	18	$ 250.00	$ 4,500.00	54	108	21.6
Year-end appeal		$ 10,000.00	$ 10,000.00			25.2
TOTAL			$100,000.00			
					Lead gift & advance gifts	80%
			80/20 rule	$72,500.00		$ 80,000.00
# of advance gift captains needed	1.92	2				
# of special gift captains needed	4.32	8				

As you can see, the chart reveals that your campaign needs 57 advance prospects that have the capacity to give between $1,500 and $10,000. The chart also reveals that you need 126 special gifts prospects who have the capacity to give between $100 and $1,000.

GREEN LIGHT
FUNDRAISING

Where are you going to find 177 people who can give between $100 and $10,000 to your nonprofit? First, remember the 80-20 rule. Eighty percent of your income is going to come from the 20% of your donors who give $1500 or more. Spend 80% of your search for prospects on the 20% who are going to give you 80% of your campaign goal.

To identify your top 20% donors, have your development assistant use your donor management software. (If your organization is new and doesn't have a history of people giving to it, don't worry; simply skip to the next section: "Adding Names to the List"). Run a couple of reports. First, run a report that identifies the donors who gave the top 20% largest one-time gifts. To do this, simply determine the number of donors on your file, and then divide by 5. Assuming you have 3,028 donors, when you divide by 5, you'll know that 20% of your donors equals 605 donors.

Then, have your assistant run a report of the number of donors who have given one-time gifts equal to or more than $100. Let's assume the report reveals that 312 people gave one-time gifts equal to or more than $100. Reduce the gift-size to equal to or more than $50. Let's assume the report reveals that 752 people gave one-time gifts equal to or more than $100. Try the report again at $60, and so on, until you have identified roughly the 600 people who gave the 20% largest one-time gifts.

Repeat the same process but this time set your donor software report to show you the top 20% of accumulative givers; i.e. not the top one-time gifts, but the top givers when you combine all the gifts each donor has given. Merge the two lists to eliminate duplicate names. You now have a list of your top 20% donors by size of gift and by accumulative giving. Print out a list of your top 20% donors.

Go through the list and mark the donors who you think have the capacity to give at the advance gifts level (from $1500 to $10,000), and those who can give at the special gifts level (from $100 to $1,000). Mark the names of donors who can't give at either level as names for your mail appeal. Your actual advance gifts and special gifts dollar levels will vary, depending on the amount of your campaign goal.

You may think, "I don't know which of our donors have the capacity to give at these levels." Don't worry. Identifying advance and special gifts prospects doesn't rest on

GREEN LIGHT
FUNDRAISING

your shoulders alone. Identify the prospects as best you can. Your work will prime the pump when you work with others on developing the prospect list.

Adding names to your list

Once you've marked all of the advance and special gifts prospects you can identify, look back over the list and then add the names at the bottom of the list of people you know in the community who have the capacity to give at the advance gifts level but who have never given before.

Ask your executive director to do the same. He or she may well recognize people on the list who have the capacity to give at a different level than you marked. Also, ask your executive director to add names at the bottom of the list of people in the community who have the capacity to give at the advance gifts level but who have never given before.

As you and your executive director look at the list, keep in mind the research that was popularized in the book, *The Millionaire Next Door*, by Thomas J. Stanley and William D. Danko. Their research revealed that the typical millionaire does not drive flashy cars and live in a penthouse.

Custom Development Solutions summarize Stanley and Dankos's findings on their website at http://www.cdsfunds.com/finding_major_gift_donors_profile_of_the_american_millionaire.html:

Profile of the Typical American Millionaire:

- 57 years old, married, 3 children
- Two-thirds are self employed
- Work (sic) 45-55 hours per week
- Median income of $131,000
- Median net worth of $1.6 million
- Modest home (half have lived in the same home for more than 20 years)
- No inheritance of funds or business
- Inexpensive clothes
- 20% are retired
- Drive (sic) 3-5 year old American made car
- Avid collectors (sic) of coupons
- Very, very frugal
- Just in case you missed the last line…Very, very frugal

GREEN LIGHT
FUNDRAISING

As I mentioned the $100,000 lead gift for the first capital campaign I directed came from a farmer who was a millionaire. He was extremely frugal. In fact, once, when we met with him, he mentioned that he had had lunch at a small town café a few days before, and that the total for his lunch came to $3.67. He fit the profile of a self-employed, frugal millionaire. He was in his 80's but he was still engaged in overseeing his farms. In fact, during the campaign he bought another farm because it was too good a deal to pass up.

What to do when your donor list does not reveal enough advance gifts prospects

You keep adding names to your list.

After you and the executive director have reviewed your top 20% donor lists and added prospects that have the capacity to give gifts at the advance level, ask key board members to do the same. Some of your board members may not have connections to people in the community who have money, but some of your board members likely will.

When you give the most connected board members clean copies of your top 20% lists to review, ask them to:

- Mark names of those who have the capacity to give at the advance gifts level;
- Initial names of any advance gifts prospects with whom they are friends;
- Initial names of any advance gifts prospects with whom they have business connections; and.
- Add names of advance gifts level prospects and initial any of the new names with whom they are friends or with whom they have business connections.

Enter the results of your survey of connected board members into your donor management database.

In all likelihood, you may still not have the 51 advance gifts prospects you need to raise $100,000. Now it's time to bring out the big guns. It's time to create a prospect committee to tap into the key people in your community who know where the money is.

   Need More Help From Rich? See p. 241    GREEN LIGHT FUNDRAISING

In every community, there are people who know where the money is, and if you guarantee them confidentiality, you will be able to gather five or six of them together to complete your list of advance gifts prospects.

Add names from other lists

But before you begin work with your prospect committee, expand your list of prospects even further. There are likely to be organizations in your town whose members are among those in the community with money. They may be members of the Chamber of Commerce. If your organization joins the Chamber, you may well have access to the membership list that you can upload to your donor management software. You may have a board member or friend of the organization who is a member of a country club or other exclusive organization who may be willing to help out your cause by supplying you with a membership list. Without identifying the source, you may add these names to your potential advance gifts givers list.

If you can't obtain the actual lists, find a member of each group who will be willing to share names with you from memory. You'll likely have to do additional research to identify addresses and phone numbers for each name.

Once you have the prospect committee convened, you can give them a clean list that includes advance gifts and special gifts donors and prospects previously identified.

Recruiting talent spotters--your prospect committee

Once you've built your advance gifts prospect list in-house, with staff and board and added names from external lists from exclusive organizations, it's time to strengthen it with the help of a group of talent-spotters—the prospect committee. As I mentioned above, every community has a few people who have a talent for knowing where the money is in the community. The secret to getting them to share that information with you for the good of your campaign is to guarantee confidentiality.

GREEN LIGHT
FUNDRAISING

I once worked on a campaign that raised funds for the mission work of a denomination. When it came time to develop a prospect list, I called up the pastors for each church. I knew that no pastor would feel comfortable serving on the prospect committee. I asked each pastor to send me a copy of their membership list. They agreed. Then, I explained that we needed to identify the people in each congregation who could give larger gifts. Then, I asked them to give me the names of two people in their congregation who would have the best handle on the giving capacity of the members of the church. Again, each pastor complied with my request.

I then called the two people from each church and described to them the missions campaign. After explaining that it was essential to know who from each church had the capacity to give sizable gifts to the campaign, I asked them to come to a prospect committee meeting. Representatives of each church would be going over their church membership list at the meeting and identifying who had the ability to give at the special gifts level and who had the ability to give at the advance gifts level.

I explained that their role would be very important to the success of the campaign but, because of the sensitive nature of their role, their involvement would be kept confidential. The prospect committee meeting went well and, later, volunteers were amazed at what a good list of prospective givers we had. More than once I was asked, "How did you get such a good list?" I indicated that a small group of confidential volunteers had helped me put the list together.

In compiling your prospect list for the advance gifts and special gifts, your goal is to do such a good job that volunteers will ask, "How did you get such a good list?"

To identify potential members of your prospect committee, ask your executive director, board and the campaign chairperson for the names of people they know who have the money in your community. Sometimes bankers or other people in the financial industry may refuse to participate, because they want to honor the confidentiality of their clients. Don't worry. You will be able to find five to six talent spotters who have a talent for knowing where the money is in your community.

Need More Help From Rich? See p. 241

GREEN LIGHT
FUNDRAISING

Ten keys to running an effective prospect committee

Here are the ten keys to running an effective prospect committee:

1. Assure confidentiality.

   The members of the prospect committee will be more willing to provide information to the campaign if they know that they will not be revealed as the source of the information

2. Prepare ahead of time the best prospect list possible.

   Your prospect committee will be able to provide you with the information efficiently you need if they start with a good list.

3. Capacity not willingness.

   Emphasize to the prospect committee that their task is to rate the names based on their capacity to give, not on their willingness to give. The prospect committee determines the capacity of prospect to give, while the willingness of a prospect is determined by their response to being asked by a volunteer.

4. Communicate the number of advance gifts prospects needed.

   You know from your gift chart the number of advance gifts prospects needed. Communicate that number to your talent spotters. Track the number of advance gifts prospects throughout the meeting so that your talent spotters will have a goal to shoot for and they will know when they achieve their goal.

5. Rate by three ranges.

   Give the committee the ranges for special gifts and advance gifts, and have them rate each name as special gifts, advance gifts, or appeal letter. The appeal letter list includes those who have the capacity to give at a level lower than the advance gifts and special gifts levels.

6. 60 to 90-minute meeting.

   People will be more likely to serve on the prospect committee if they know that their time will be respected and the meeting will last no more than 60-90 minutes.

GREEN LIGHT
FUNDRAISING

7. Recorder.

To make the meeting productive, it's helpful for the development director or development assistant to record the input of the committee. Use three different color highlighters, using one color to highlight special gifts, a second color to highlight the advance gifts, and a third color to highlight the appeal letter level gifts.

8. Keep the meeting moving.

Keeping the volunteers on track to rate quickly the names requires a tactful facilitator. The role can be played by one of the volunteers on the prospect committee, the executive director, or the development director. It's important to name the facilitator ahead of time and coach them to keep the process moving.

9. Add names.

Have the committee members add names, especially names of advance gifts prospects that have previously been overlooked.

10. Thank the prospect committee members.

When the volunteers have completed the task of rating the names, thank them and assure them that they have played an important role in making the campaign a success.

Tips for getting to know advance gifts prospects

Your lead and advance gifts prospects will provide 80% of the income to your campaign. Given their importance to your organization, you want to know as much as possible about each advance gifts prospect to increase the likelihood of his or her giving. Information about an advance gifts prospect will help develop a positive relationship between that prospect and your organization. Knowledge and friendships increase the likelihood of the prospect becoming a donor who gives generously year after year.

GREEN LIGHT
FUNDRAISING

Here's additional information that will help the people soliciting with the advance gifts prospects:

- Identify all connections with your organization
- Past or present board members;
- Past or present committee members;
- Past employees. A friend and I worked as vocational counselors at same nonprofit when we were just out of college. He went on to become CEO of a major snowmobile manufacturer;
- Family members of those who have received services. This is perhaps the most powerful connection between a nonprofit and a potential donor;
- Friends of board, staff, or committee members; and
- Other connections.

Signs a prospect may give.

Perhaps you have someone in your community who you know has never given to your organization. You can still look for signs that a prospect may be willing to give such as:

- Given to similar causes;
- Served as a volunteer or board member for an organization similar to yours; and
- Friends with someone whose family has benefited from your organization's services.
- Hobbies and other interests.

When I was a nonprofit human resources director, I went to training on interviewing people. The trainer told the story of a job placement service that regularly sent applicants for interviews to a certain company. They had discovered that the interviewer was an avid fisherman. They began to coach applicants to bring up the topic of fishing during the interview and their placement rate at that company went up significantly.

GREEN LIGHT
FUNDRAISING

Remember the principles of persuasion highlighted in chapter 11? Principle 5:"People prefer to say yes to your request to the degree that they know and like you. No surprise there." We tend to like people who share our interests.

Looking ahead

You've now learned the keys to recruiting volunteers and the secrets to creating a great prospect list for your volunteer solicitors. Now it's time to learn a simple and powerful tool to tap into the innate motivation of your volunteers to do a good job of raising funds for your organization.

How can we improve?

E-mail us at (comment@greenlightfundraising.org) to let us know when something is unclear, or you have a suggestion for improving the book. Please identify the page and paragraph that needs improving.

CHAPTER 15

Scorecards: Tapping Into Your Volunteers'
Motivation for Mastery

My daughter, Hannah, wrote eight grant applications as she was growing a mental wellness program for seniors. Seven times, her grant applications were rejected. Her eighth application was funded to the tune of $300,000 a year for three years, with the possibility of extending it to five years.

Suddenly she had to hire several staff members and a coordinator for the program. Exciting times.

But several months into the program, she realized she had trouble on her hands. The new coordinator and staff were emphasizing one part of the program and neglecting other parts of the program. When my daughter pointed out the areas that they were neglecting, she met resistance.

She called me for a consultation. I listened to the issues as she outlined them. As always in workplace conflicts, the human resources issues were complex. Over time, she was going to have to deal with the hiring mistakes she had made.

But I didn't focus on the human resources issues since her supervisors and human resources department would help her deal with them.

Instead, I suggested she create a scorecard.

I pointed out that, when she had written the grant, she had made commitments, promising the funder that her organization would carry out certain activities and achieve certain results. I suggested that she translate those commitments into a scorecard so that she and her staff were clear how they were doing on these promises to the funder. I suggested that the scorecard be updated every week so that she and her staff could, together, track their progress.

She created a scorecard and she and her staff began to review it every week. Gradually, the scorecard helped her and her staff to be on the same page. Not only did it put the team on the same page but it helped her individual staff members to master their job. A couple of years later the scorecard won 2nd place in a statewide Best Practices Recognition Program for her industry.

 Need More Help From Rich? See p. 241  GREEN LIGHT FUNDRAISING

Besides keeping your team on track towards the campaign goal, scorecards provide valuable information that your volunteers can use to master asking for gifts

What motivates your volunteers?

As a nonprofit leader, you have no carrots and no sticks to motivate your volunteers. Employers have carrots and sticks, but nonprofits do not employ volunteers.

Here's the good news: science shows that carrots and sticks do not work for tasks as complicated as asking someone for a gift.

It's almost universally accepted in the business world that commissions are a carrot, a good way to motivate salespeople. In the world of fundraising consulting, paying the consultant commissions based on the amount of money raised is considered unethical. Which is the better way to go? Is it the business world with its sales bonuses, or the nonprofit consulting world with no bonuses?

Executives at Redgate, a British software company, grew tired of creating commission systems because sales people always figured out a way to game the system. Also, they realized that the commission system was based on a false assumption about people— that they are "fundamentally inert and passive" and that if they didn't have a carrot in front of us or a stick behind them, they wouldn't do anything. "Human nature," Daniel Pink said in a presentation to a 250 year-old organization, the Royal Society for the Encouragement of Arts, Manufactures and Commerce (RSA), "is to be active and engaged." Look at any two year-old. Look at four year-olds. They are active and engaged.

Redgate eliminated the commissions on sales. What happened? Sales increased because sales people became more collaborative with each other. In addition, management spent less time policing their sales force and more time helping customers.

If financial carrots don't motivate your volunteers, what does?

As you think about the motivation of your volunteers, I suggest that you consider two studies commissioned by the Federal Reserve Bank and reported on by Daniel Pink in his presentation to the RSA.

GREEN LIGHT
FUNDRAISING

Traditionally, Pink says, we have thought that people are motivated by rewards and punishment, i.e. the carrot and the stick. These two studies, one done in the USA with college students and the other done in a rural area of India, showed that monetary rewards work on mechanical tasks like putting a ball in a basket, but do not work for tasks that require even a rudimentary cognitive skill, like memorizing a string of numbers. In fact, a larger monetary reward led to poorer performance with both the USA college students and impoverished people in rural India.

Pink concludes the following from the studies: "When a task gets more complicated--it requires some conceptual, creative thinking--rewards demonstrably do not work."

The only time money is an issue is if you pay people too little and they think their pay is unfair. But if you pay people enough, they stop thinking about money and focus on the work. In the case of volunteers, no one feels that the pay is unfair, because no one expects to be paid.

There are three things that motivate people, including volunteers, to do a good job. These are the three things that lead to better performance and more personal satisfaction when comes to challenging, cognitive tasks:

- Autonomy;
- Mastery; and
- Purpose.

Autonomy is the desire to be self-directed. I grew up among farmers who took great pride in being their own boss. It turns out that being self-directed is very motivating. For instance, every three months an Australian software company, Atlassian, gives its workers 24 hours to work on whatever they want. All they have to do is report the results at an informal gathering afterwards. That one day a quarter of autonomy has led to all kinds of software fixes and new products.

Mastery is the urge to improve. That's why people play musical instruments evenings and weekends. They want to get better.

 Need More Help From Rich? See p. 241  GREEN LIGHT FUNDRAISING

Purpose is the desire to make a contribution. More and more businesses are trying to create a transcendent purpose for their existence, because people like to work for companies that are making the world a better place. For instance, the founder of Skype says, "Our goal is to be destructive but in the cause of making the world a better place."

The whole open source software movement is based on autonomy, mastery and purpose. Software people around the world have freely given of their time to create open source products like the Linux operating system which is used by one out of four Fortune 500 companies, Apache, which powers a majority of web servers, and the powerful online encyclopedia, Wikipedia. You can watch "The Surprising Truth about What Motivates Us," an RSA animation that highlights the key points in Pink's presentation, in an 10-minute video at http://www.youtube.com/watch?v=u6XAPnuFjJc. You can see the full 41-minute presentation at http://www.thersa.org/events/vision/vision-videos/dan-pink-drive.

A fundraising campaign provides plenty of room for all three motivators. Volunteers have autonomy as to when and where they meet with potential givers. They have autonomy in choosing with whom they will meet.

Volunteers have the opportunity for mastery, for getting better at asking people for money.

Volunteers have an opportunity to make a contribution to their community by raising funds that will help transform the lives of people on the edges of your community.

Your challenge as a development director is to support all three motivations. You've already built autonomy for your volunteers, allowing them to select from whom they raise funds and where and when they ask for a gift. And you've already built a transcendent purpose into your campaign through the stories of transformed lives.

Let's look at one more tool that you can use to tap into your volunteers' desire for mastery.

GREEN LIGHT
FUNDRAISING

Mastery with scorecards

In chapter 16, you will learn how to teach your volunteers the art of the GOOD way of asking for a gift. In addition to learning how to ask for a gift, you will teach them to use "The successful ask checklist," a tool that will keep them focused on the steps they need to follow in order to ask successfully for a gift.

There's a second tool that can help volunteers master the art of asking for gifts—the scorecard.

A basketball scorecard keeps the individuals on a team focused on the short-term goals as well as the end goal, of winning the game. In basketball, the scorecard tracks such short-term goals as three pointers, field goals, free throws, assists, turnovers, fouls, and rebounds, while the scoreboard keeps track of the total points scored by each team.

The players and everyone in the gym can see the scoreboard, but the scorecard with the detailed stats is a tool used primarily by the coaches who want to help their team master all aspects of the game.

Usually everyone in the gym knows who's scoring the most points for each team during a game; however, coaches know that the final score is a result not only of shooting, but on lesser known stats like how well individuals on a team are performing on rebounding and assists.

Designing a scorecard to encourage mastery in your volunteers

Encouraging mastery among your volunteers is essential to creating a sustainable campaign. Frontline volunteers who feel like they are learning and growing in their ability to ask for gifts will be eager to volunteer year after year. I suggest you design a smart and friendly system called a scorecard that focuses on the performance of each volunteer and will give volunteers the feedback they need to master asking for gifts. Here's an example based on gift chart 2 in chapter 12:

 Need More Help From Rich? See p. 241  GREEN LIGHT FUNDRAISING

Campaign volunteer advance gifts scorecard

Advance gifts goal: $57,500				% of calls	
	# cards taken	# of calls made	% cards called on	# gifts rc'd	leading to gift	Total gifts rc'd
Brookes	5	5	100%	3	60%	$13,000.00
Dunn	5	3	60%	2	67%	$ 5,000.00
John	5	5	100%	3	60%	$ 7,000.00
Paul	6	6	100%	5	83%	$17,000.00
George	5	3	60%	3	100%	$ 4,500.00
Ringo	5	2	40%	1	50%	$ 5,000.00
Loretta	5	4	80%	3	75%	$ 3,250.00
Taylor	6	5	83%	5	100%	$10,650.00
						$65,400.00

As you can see, the scorecard above contains valuable, detailed information that volunteers can use to improve their mastery of asking for gifts.

You can use the scorecard in two ways. First, for high-performing volunteers, you may include a scorecard with the volunteer's stats in your thank letter to him or her. You can thank the person for volunteering, point out the highlights of his or her individual scorecard, and invite the person to consider keeping up their great stats next year.

Second, you discuss the scorecard with the advance gifts chairperson as part of his or her orientation, and discuss possible ways to recognize your volunteers.

You can adapt the scorecard above for use with your special gifts phase also. You can find a sample Excel spreadsheet used to produce the scorecard above on the Green Light Fundraising website at http://greenlightfundraising.org/downloads/scorecard. xls.

GREEN LIGHT
FUNDRAISING

Designing a scoreboard for the public

While a scorecard has detailed information on the performance of each team member, it's helpful to have a scoreboard that tracks the progress of the campaign towards its overall goal.

Traditionally, campaigns have used an outline of a thermometer with dollar levels painted on a white board as a visual scoreboard for the public, with the ultimate goal at the top of the thermometer. Usually, the thermometer is posted outside the nonprofit or at another prominent location in the community. As the campaign progresses, someone from the nonprofit paints in the thermometer and everyone can see the progress toward the goal. You need something akin to a thermometer to track overall progress.

You can use creative variations of the thermometer concept like a nonprofit I worked for did for its holiday campaign, the Tree of Hope (a direct mail campaign that I describe in more detail in Chapter 18). As the campaign progressed, we lit a large Christmas tree located near the street in front of our building, from the bottom up, making the lighting of the Tree of Hope was our variation on the thermometer concept.

Check the theme for your campaign or your organization's logo to see if your can create an alternative to the thermometer concept that fits with your nonprofit and campaign.

Designing a gift chart dashboard for your e-letter update

The success of your campaign depends on 80-20 rule. A mentioned in Chapter 5, fundraisers began to build on the 80-20 rule by creating a gift chart that shows the number of gifts needed at each level to achieve a goal, with a distribution of 80% of the total coming from 20% of the donors, and 20% of the goal coming from 80% of the donors.

While the reality of the distribution of gifts never fits exactly with the gift chart, it's helpful to create a gift chart dashboard to communicate what level of gifts have come in and what level of gifts are still needed.

When I first described my vision for a dashboard to my assistant at the time, Gina Goggio, she talked it over with her accountant husband and he recommended we use the stackable bar chart feature of an Excel spreadsheet.

Need More Help From Rich? See p. 241
GREEN LIGHT
FUNDRAISING

Below is a sample of a gift chart dashboard showing the completion of the advance gifts phase of a $100,000 campaign using the data from the advance gifts scorecard above. The special gifts phase and the direct mail phase are still to take place. The green bars show funds that have been received from each gift chart level. The red bars show how much is still needed in each gift chart level. Here's the graph:

To create the dashboard above we used the following data:

Size of Gift	Received	Goal
$ 15,000	$15,000	$0
$ 10,000	$10,000	$0
$ 7,500	$15,000	$0
$ 5,000	$15,000	$0
$ 2,500	$12,500	$0
$ 1,500	$7,500	$0
$ 1,000	$2,000	$6,000
$ 500	$3,250	$1,750
$ 250	$150	$4,350
$100 & under		$10,000
	$80,400	$22,100

GREEN LIGHT
FUNDRAISING

Column 1, the size of gifts (taken from the gift chart), shows up as the slanted labels at the bottom of the bar graph. Column 2 represents the amount received of each size of gift, and shows up as green in each bar in the above dashboard. Column 3 represents the amount left to be raised to meet the goal for each size gift and shows up as a red bar.

You can find a sample Excel spreadsheet used to produce the dashboard above on the Evergreen Green Light Fundraising website at http://greenlightfundraising.org/downloads/dashboard.xls.

Looking ahead

You are now ready to learn the most critical task in fundraising—asking for the gift. In the first 15 chapters you learned how to create the case for your cause, market your campaign, recruit the volunteer leaders and solicitors, create a powerful prospect list, and handle umpteen details for a successful campaign.

Now it's time to learn how to teach your eager volunteers the GOOD way to ask for the gift.

How can we improve?

E-mail us at (comment@greenlightfundraising.org) to let us know when something is unclear, or you have a suggestion for improving the book. Please identify the page and paragraph that needs improving.

Need More Help From Rich? See p. 241

GREEN LIGHT
FUNDRAISING

CHAPTER 16

The GOOD Way To Ask

There is one reason to ask for money for a community nonprofit—to transform lives.

Not everyone believes this. One day earlier in my career, I excitedly called a friend and told her that I was being recruited to direct a campaign to raise $600,000. She laughed and said, "That sounds like the kind of job anyone foolish enough to accept could have."

Fundraising is not a high status job. I've never heard of a child saying, "I want to grow up to be a fundraiser." In fact, you may have been disciplined as a child for fund raising . . .er, begging. . . a quarter off a generous uncle.

Recently I was at a financial advisory team meeting of a membership nonprofit. Their income had been flat for several years. Then they had received a bequest, hired staff, burned through the bequest, laid off staff, and were back to their flat line income.

Even though I was there as a volunteer (since a nonprofit I'm part of is a member organization) I said, "I'm going to put on my consultant hat." Then I suggested that they consider a new model of fundraising that included raising funds from individuals, as well as their long-established practice of raising funds from their membership organizations. I knew I was treading on sensitive ground because when you suggest a change to a well-established organizational model, you are inviting resistance.

I had been on the financial advisory team long enough to know that the director did not have the time to take on sustainable fundraising. I suggested that they hire a part-time development director to lead the effort to raise funds from individuals, indicating that the director would have his role to play in sustainable fundraising.

The director had been in his position for a year, but he was still resistant to my suggestion. The resistance emerged in two forms. First, he said, "I do not want to go begging." Second, he said, "I do not even like the word 'fundraising.' There has to be a better word."

"There are a lot of fundraisers who don't like the word 'fundraiser,'" I acknowledged. "That's why they use titles like 'director of development.' Perhaps it's the stubborn side of me but a long time ago I decided to proudly use the word 'fundraiser' to describe what I do.

Need More Help From Rich? See p. 241

GREEN LIGHT
FUNDRAISING

"Fundraising is not begging," I continued. "People do not give to a nonprofit because you beg them to, but because of the lives that are transformed by the work of the nonprofit."

Getting a little emotional, I said, "I have had the honor of seeing many lives transformed through my work as a fundraiser."

The director and I went on to have a very fruitful discussion. I came to understand that he had a real passion for increasing income from the member organizations. At the same time, he pushed me to describe sustainable fundraising and how it might work for their organization. In the end, we both agreed that it made sense for him to ramp up his efforts to increase income from member organizations for a year, and then consider sustainable fundraising.

Beggars get quarters and dollars. As a fundraising professional, you need to raise tens of thousands, and perhaps hundreds of thousands of dollars every year to transforms lives.

You can name the names of people and, in your minds-eye, see the faces of people whose lives have taken a dramatic turn for the better because of the work of your nonprofit.

Your challenge as a development director (or executive director or volunteer campaign director, if your organization does not have a development director) is to teach volunteers—people who do not work every day for your nonprofit--how to ask for gifts in a positive, powerful way that helps them overcome the natural fears that are part of asking.

Your challenge is to help your volunteers to catch enough of the passion and knowledge that you have, to allow them to be successful in doing their part in transforming lives through the work of your nonprofit.

This chapter teaches you how to capture the imagination of your volunteers as you teach them to transform lives by asking for gifts through a simple, powerful and effective step-be-step approach.

Remember, there is one reason to raise money—to transform lives.

GREEN LIGHT
FUNDRAISING

It take's leadership skills and a heart

It's no surprise that it's the leaders of a community who head up fundraising campaigns. It takes leaders to get things done. Every volunteer who serves in your campaign is a leader. They serve not because they are beggars, but because they are leaders who have both leadership skills and a heart to use those skills to transform the lives of the people your nonprofit serves.

When you train volunteers on how to ask, you need to give them the message that you know they have volunteered because they are a leader with a heart.

Giving and receiving money is a leadership skill and can be honed like any other skill. There is a skill to asking. I call it the GOOD way of transforming lives through giving and receiving. GOOD is an acronym for:

Give Generously Yourself;

Opportunity to Make a Difference;

Open with a Story; and

Defer to and Respect the Person.

Note

Be sure to emphasize to your volunteer solicitors in the advance gifts and special gifts phases that they are expected to meet and ask for gifts in-person, not through a letter or a phone call. Tell them fundraisers have discovered that if you want to raise a little money, send a letter; and if you want to raise a little more money, make a phone call; and if you want to raise a lot of money, ask in person. In both the advance gifts and special gifts phases the campaign goal requires us to raise a lot of money, thus, it is essential that volunteers ask in person.

GREEN LIGHT
FUNDRAISING

Give generously yourself

When I teach a group of volunteers to ask for gifts, I make sure that I have made my own generous gift or pledge to the campaign before I begin the training.

Why?

Leaders lead by getting out front. I cannot honestly and passionately lead others to ask for money unless I have given first. I need to be upfront in my giving. I mention to the volunteers that I have already given generously because I want them to do the same.

The first step to asking for money is to give generously yourself. The first crank of the wheel to fulfill successfully your role in helping the campaign succeed in transforming lives is to give generously yourself.

When you give generously, you will be able to use that highly influential Cialdini principle: "People will be likely to say yes to your request if you give them evidence that people just like them have been saying yes to it."

What is generous? The best rule of thumb is to ask each volunteer to give in the range in which they are volunteering. Advance gifts volunteers should give in the advance gifts range and special gifts volunteers in the special gifts range.

Encourage them to look at the range of gifts needed in the phase of the campaign for which they are volunteering and then let their heart be their guide. They know their finances. No one else does. Tell them, "Keep trying out numbers on yourself until you land on one that your heart says, 'Now that's a generous gift/pledge that I can do.'"

As Reynold Levy, President of the Lincoln Center for the Performing Arts, says in his book, *Yours for the Asking*, "When asking someone you know for a gift to charity, no argument is more convincing than citing your own donation, and no words more compelling than 'please join me.'" (Levy, Reynold. John Wiley & Sons, Hoboken, New Jersey, 2008, p. 39)

GREEN LIGHT
FUNDRAISING

Opportunity to make a difference

After I completed graduate school in counseling in 1977, I couldn't find a job as a counselor. After a couple of months, I took a job as a personnel director at Horizon House of Illinois Valley, an organization that provided work and living services for adults with developmental disabilities.

I assumed that I would be there a few months and then would move on to a better job. A funny thing happened. A few months into the job, I began to realize that the organization was making a tremendous difference in the lives of the people that it served. A few years later I switched to the director of development position. I put in twenty years as a staff member at HH, then became a fundraising consultant, and eventually launched Evergreen Leaders.

Whether working as a nonprofit staff member or consulting with clients, the juice that keeps me going is the opportunity to make a difference in the lives of people whose lives are transformed by the work of nonprofits.

When you train volunteers to ask for gifts for your nonprofit, you are giving them the opportunity to make a difference.

When I studied social work as an undergraduate and counseling as a graduate student, I assumed that I would make a difference by helping people. A few months into my job at HHIV, I discovered that I loved administrative work. At first, I felt guilty. After all, I wasn't working directly with the people whom the nonprofit served; I wasn't "helping people."

One day, I confessed my love of administrative work, and my guilt about not really helping people to an older and wiser friend who happened to be a direct service worker at HH. She cut through my youthful confusion with a simple observation: "We need good administrators too."

GREEN LIGHT
FUNDRAISING

From then on, I embraced my work as personnel director and, later, as a fundraiser, with a new attitude. I began to see my work as an opportunity to make a difference by fulfilling the needs that direct service workers have for good administrators and for funds to do their work of transforming lives.

When you ask for a gift, there is an ocean of difference between having the attitude of the beggar and the attitude of the person who is offering someone the opportunity to make a difference.

The attitude of the beggar is one of being fearful, self-centered and desperate, because a beggar is focused on the money he needs for his next meal or fix. The attitude of your volunteer fundraisers will be courage, confidence and a focus on how exciting it is to offer a potential donor a chance to participate in the work of transforming lives. As Thomas Jefferson said, "Nothing can stop the man with the right mental attitude from achieving his goal; nothing on earth can help the man with the wrong mental attitude."

> The attitude of your volunteer fundraisers will be courage, confidence and focus on how exciting it is to offer the potential donor a chance to participate in the work of transforming lives.

With the right attitude, the volunteer can confidently call each of the five people they have committed to asking for a gift and say, "I'm working on a project for a nonprofit, _____, and I'd like to meet with you over coffee to talk about it. When would be a good time for you and I to get together?"

Remember the Heath brothers six principles of making ideas stick that we covered in Chapter 5? Ideas that stick are concrete. As the camapign director, you need concrete stories that show how your nonprofit transforms lives. Concrete means sensory. "Naturally sticky ideas are full of concrete images— ice-filled bathtubs, apples with razors — because our brains are wired to remember concrete data," the Heath brothers wrote.

As part of training your volunteers how to ask, tell a concrete story of someone's life who is being transformed by your nonprofit, or whose life may be transformed by the work of your nonprofit. Again, you may need to change any identifying details to protect the person's identity.

GREEN LIGHT
FUNDRAISING

Better yet, have someone who has benefited from your organization tell his or her story, or create a short video of someone describing how their life was transformed by the work of your nonprofit.

The point of the story is to help your volunteers understand at a deep level that they have an opportunity to transform lives through your nonprofit by their work of raising funds.

When a volunteer sits down with a person to ask him or her for a gift, you want that volunteer to feel, at a deep level, that he or she is offering the person the opportunity to transform lives through a gift.

In your training at the kickoff, volunteers will be able to look around the room and see that people just like them are eager to make a difference by asking others to give. By the time you do the training in the advance gifts kickoff and special gifts kickoff, you will know how many volunteers have committed to ask for gifts. Remind the volunteers of the number of people who volunteered to raise x amount of dollars for your nonprofit during the campaign. Emphasize that each of these volunteers will be asking people to make gifts to make a difference in the lives of people like those whose stories they have just heard.

Open with a story

Your volunteers are going to want to know the answer to this question: "What do I say to the person when I sit down with them?"

Your answer? After "How are you doing?", "What are your kids up to?," and the opening chit chat, when you sense it's time to get down to business, open your presentation by telling a story about why the work of the nonprofit is important to you.

> Enthusiasm is a great way to counter the natural fear that one has in asking for a gift.

Many volunteers will feel comfortable in telling their own story—the story about why they agreed to volunteer for the campaign. They may know someone who benefited from the nonprofit's work. They may know someone on the board or the staff who is passionate about the work of the nonprofit. They may have picked up a story from one of these people that they can tell as a concrete way of communicating the good work that your nonprofit does.

Need More Help From Rich? See p. 241

GREEN LIGHT
FUNDRAISING

Or they may say, "I didn't know anything about the work of this nonprofit, but Joe called me up and, you know Joe, he's hard to say no to. So I agreed to volunteer to ask five people for gifts for the campaign. And since I volunteered, I've learned a lot more about the work of this organization." Then the volunteer can tell one of the stories they have read in the case statement or a story from the kickoff.

Encourage your volunteers to think ahead of time through the story they will tell. Then, practice their story. Keep practicing their story until they get excited about it. Winston Churchill said, "There is in that act of preparing, the moment you start caring." You want your volunteers to care about the great work that your nonprofit does, and they will care as they develop their own story.

Some of your volunteers will be veterans in asking for money. Don't worry. Teach them anyway, and they are sure to learn something from the GOOD way of asking for gifts.

Encourage your volunteers to be openly enthusiastic as they tell their story. Enthusiasm is a great way to counter the natural fear that one has in asking for a gift. Once your volunteers are confident in the story they have to tell, they will be enthusiastic. Enthusiasm is contagious and people who catch your enthusiasm are likely to give generously.

Encourage your volunteers to weave into their story the goal for this year's campaign and the progress being made on the campaign.

Have your volunteers conclude their story with, "And that's just one example of how your gift and mine will transform lives through the work of this organization."

A good story equals the ability to be enthusiastic and persuasive.

Defer to and respect the person

When you ask someone for money. the most important time is not when you begin talking but when you stop. It's that moment just after you've asked for $100,000.

Or asked for $100.

GREEN LIGHT
FUNDRAISING

If your volunteers have followed the GOOD way of asking for a gift, at this stage they have led by giving generously themselves, they have seen their conversation with the potential donor as offering the person the opportunity to transform lives through a gift to your nonprofit, and they've told a concrete story about how the nonprofit transforms lives.

Now is the time for each volunteer to ask the question. The ideal is for each volunteer to ask for a specific amount, especially volunteers in the advance gifts phase.

Here's the model question for your volunteers to ask for the gift: "Hannah, as you can tell, this organization is doing great work. Will you consider a gift of $5,000?"

Then stop talking. Wait until the person answers before you say anything.

Defer in silence to the person. If you speak first, you interrupt the hard work the person is doing as they think about whether to give a gift and how much.

You may be very tempted to speak. Don't. When I teach volunteers how to ask, sales people brighten up at the point. They know that at this moment in the conversation, silence is golden. One volunteer said to me, "My Dad was in sales and he used to say, 'The first one who speaks, loses.'"

Wait.

Then accept the answer. Some will say yes. When the campaign chairperson and I met with the first lead gift prospect for the campaign that underwrote the writing and production of this ebook, we asked for $5,000. She said yes. And then she explained that she had looked at her finances before meeting with us and had concluded that she could make a gift of $5,000.

Some will say no. We've planned for the reality that some people will say no by identifying three prospects for every gift we need.

Some will say they need more time to think about it.

If she says she needs more time to think about it, or to discuss it with her husband, ask her how long she needs. When she tells you, tell her you'll call her then to get her decision.

Whatever the answer, if you follow the steps of the GOOD way of asking, you can be assured that you have done your best to make a difference.

Not all volunteers are going to feel comfortable asking for a specific amount. I've developed an alternative approach for such people. I encourage them to show the gift chart to the potential donors and point to the advance gifts range. Explain that the gift chart shows the number of gifts needed at each level in order for the campaign to succeed. People often prefer a choice in their giving, and by asking for a gift within a range, you give them a choice.

Here's the model question for your volunteers who prefer to ask for the gift within a range rather than a specific amount: "Hannah, as you can tell, this is an organization that changes lives. Will you consider a gift in the upper advance gifts range?"

Then stop talking and follow the steps outlined above.

The final word on the GOOD way of asking

Practice.

Practice how you are going to teach your volunteers the GOOD way of asking, and encourage your volunteers to practice the GOOD way of asking.

Several years ago, I had a good friend who was starting work as a peacemaker in Colombia. He needed to raise funds, and he was new to fundraising. He practiced his phone calls with me on the phone, and he practiced his in-person presentations with me in person. And he raised all the money he's needed each year since.

Wrapping up your training with a checklist

You've just taught your volunteers how to ask. Taken individually, each step is simple but together they can be overwhelming to first-time fundraisers. And even if they remember the steps, will they follow them?

GREEN LIGHT
FUNDRAISING

Take heart from the work of a physician, Peter Pronovost, who works full time in the Johns Hopkins Hospital. A New Yorker article (http://tinyurl.com/yvp6l9) chronicles how, in 2001, he began to wonder if a checklist would help the ICU to do a better job of preventing infections that are often associated with inserting lines in patients.

There are five simple steps to prevent an infection while putting in a line. These steps are routinely taught and are well known to ICU doctors. Pronovost created a checklist with the five steps and asked the nurses in the ICU to complete the checklist each time the doctors inserted lines to assess how well they followed these well-known procedures. The nurses did the checklists for a month.

At the end of a month, the checklists revealed that the doctors missed at least one step in more than one- third of the patients.

The next month Pronovost persuaded the administrators to authorize the nurses to stop the doctors if they missed a step on the checklist:

> Pronovost and his colleagues monitored what happened for a year afterward. The results were so dramatic that they weren't sure whether to believe them: the ten-day line-infection rate went from eleven per cent to zero. So they followed patients for fifteen more months. Only two line infections occurred during the entire period. They calculated that, in this one hospital, the checklist had prevented forty-three infections and eight deaths, and saved two million dollars in costs.

While your volunteer fundraisers are not handling life and death situations like ICU doctors, they are doing work that will transform the lives of individuals in your communities. And they will want to do their best. You can help them do their best with a simple checklist. The checklist will do two things. First, it will help the volunteers remember the steps to asking for a gift successfully. Two, it will give you feedback on how useful the steps are.

Nonprofits thrive not only on compassion and good people, but on smart and friendly systems like checklists.

GREEN LIGHT
FUNDRAISING

You are likely to get resistance from your volunteers regarding "more paperwork." Tell them the story of Dr. Pronovost saving eight lives in two years and three months with the use of a simple checklist. You only have the power of stories and friendly persuasion to get the checklists completed. Do your best.

You want to master the art of asking people to make a gift to a good cause. We want to master the art of teaching people how to ask for gifts for a good cause.

To help you achieve mastery in asking for gifts and us to achieve mastery in teaching volunteers to ask, we've created a checklist. Here it is:

The successful ask checklist

Volunteer _____ Potential Donor_____

1. I successfully arranged for a face-to-face conversation. ___Yes ___No

2. I made my own generous gift before meeting with the potential donor.
   ___Yes ___No

3. I told the potential donor the story (check one):

   i.   Of a life transformed by the work of my nonprofit ___Yes ___No

   ii. Of how I came to volunteer for my nonprofit ___Yes ___No

   iii. I skipped this part ___Yes ___No

4. I asked for:

   i.   _____ a specific amount ___Yes ___No

   ii. _____ a gift within a range ___Yes ___No

   iii. _____ didn't ask for a specific amount ___Yes ___No

5. After I asked for the gift, I deferred in silence until the donor prospect responded. ___Yes ___No

6. _____ Amount donated

GREEN LIGHT
FUNDRAISING

You will find a checklist for the steps to successfully asking for a gift on the Green Light Fundraising website at http://greenlightfundraising.org/downloads/askchecklist.doc.

Remember, there is one reason to raise money—to transform lives.

Looking ahead

Now that you've learned how to teach your great volunteers how to ask for gifts, it's time to learn how to plan and execute a kickoff for each solicitation phase. It's during the kickoff that you train your volunteers to ask for gifts. Your volunteers' time is precious. You want to honor their time, and in the next chapter you will learn how to plan each kickoff and to execute it in an hour or less.

How can we improve?

E-mail us at (comment@greenlightfundraising.org) to let us know when something is unclear, or you have a suggestion for improving the book. Please identify the page and paragraph that needs improving.

Page 200

Need More Help From Rich? See p. 241

GREEN LIGHT
FUNDRAISING

CHAPTER 17

Kickoffs: Let The Fun Begin

On Memorial Day weekend 2003, nine of us from Indiana, Illinois, and Iowa, gathered at Plow Creek, the religious community I am part of, to found Evergreen Leaders. Toward the end of the two-day meeting, as a symbol of the beginning of this new venture, we planted a Colorado blue spruce seedling.

At the end of the two-day kickoff of this new, fledgling nonprofit, I was exhilarated. It fulfilled a dream - a call - that I had been sensing for years.

> Nourish beginnings, let us nourish beginnings. Not all things are blest, but the seeds of all things are blest. The blessing is in the seed.
>
> – Muriel Rukeyser

When we planted the Colorado blue spruce, it was about eight inches tall. The tag on the tree said that it would grow to be 35 feet tall. Now, seven years later, it is six feet tall and still growing.

There is joy in beginnings.

When you launch your first sustainable fundraising campaign, you are planting a seed that may seem small at the beginning, but it will grown and, over time, raise a huge amount of money to help transform lives in your nonprofit.

Like the founding of Evergreen Leaders, your first sustainable campaign will be fragile and yet full of promise. The first time you kickoff the solicitation phase of your sustainable fundraising drive, you may have a dry mouth. Will this really work?

I have another favorite quote about beginnings:

> *Let us watch well our beginnings, and results will manage themselves.*
>
> *Alexander Clark*

As the campaign director (whether it is in your role as development director or, if your organization doesn't have a development director, you may be campaign director by virtue of being executive director or a volunteer), your task is to watch well the beginnings—the kickoffs of each phase. In Chapter 16, we covered teaching volunteers the GOOD way of asking for a gift, an essential element to the kickoff. In Chapter 13, we focused on the Inner Circle phases where board and staff are invited to participate in the campaign. This chapter provides information on how to structure the advance gifts and special gifts phase kickoffs.

GREEN LIGHT
FUNDRAISING

Advance Gifts Kickoff or How to Launch the Quiet Phase

For a campaign to be successful, you want to build momentum and keep that momentum going until the wrap-up celebration. The first stage of building momentum begins with the lead gift. Securing the lead gift builds tremendous momentum.

The second stage of building momentum is the advance gifts stage. It's called the quiet phase because it happens before the media blitz that is essential to help the special gifts phase to put you over the top of your goal. You want to have raised 60% to 80% of your goal before you go public with the launch of the special gifts phase, also known as the public phase.

When the advance gifts phase hits its goal, it builds tremendous momentum for the final phase of the campaign.

Preparing for the Advance Gifts Kickoff

You have three options for scheduling the advance gifts kickoff—before work in the morning, at noon, or immediately after work. Your advance gifts chairperson will have a sense of which time will work best for his or her team.

Depending on the time of day the event is scheduled, provide an appropriate snack, light meal, and coffee or soda.

Prior to the kickoff, the development staff should create a prospect card for each advance gifts prospect. You can find sample prospect cards on the Green Light Fundraising website at http://greenlightfundraising.org/downloads/prospect1.pdf

http://greenlightfundraising.org/downloads/prospect2.doc.

Before the kickoff begins, lay out the prospect cards in alphabetical order on a table. As part of the advance gifts packet for the kickoff, provide a complete alphabetical list of the advance gifts prospects and a compete alphabetical list of the special gifts prospects.

Prepare a packet for each advance gifts team member. You may print some the items in the packet on different colored paper stock to make it easy for team members to find the document to which you are referring. For instance, you might print the

GREEN LIGHT
FUNDRAISING

advance gifts prospect list on light blue stock and the special gifts prospect list on light yellow stock.

The packet should include the following:

- Agenda for the advance gifts kickoff ;
- The volunteer's prospect card;
- Five "Successful Ask Check Lists";
- Sample advance gifts team score card;
- Case statement;
- Five campaign brochures;
- If available, a press clipping or two about your organization;
- Organization's brochure(s);
- Advance gifts prospect list;
- Special gifts prospect list; and
- Other documents such as an annual report or the organization's IRS letter affirming your 501c3 status (especially if your nonprofit is in the start-up phase and not well-known in your community).

The secret to each volunteer achieving 20% of their goal on the first day

The success of your campaign depends on every volunteer soliciting five people. Your stars will solicit more than five people, but you will not know who your stars are your first-year, so be a stickler about the five card rule. During the training you can tell your first-year volunteers that some of them will be stars. How will you know that they will be stars? They will promptly meet with their five prospects and obtain three to four gifts and then they will come back and ask for more cards. Those are the stars.

More on the five card rule.

Learn from my mistake and stick to the five card rule. Once, I was consulting with a campaign and one of the volunteers was an insurance agent who seemed to know everyone. He selected twenty cards. How many people did he contact?

One.

Need More Help From Rich? See p. 241

GREEN LIGHT
FUNDRAISING

Why? Because I let him break the five card rule. He was overwhelmed with the idea of meeting with twenty prospects, and after one call he became discouraged and gave up. He lost momentum because I had let him proclaim he could run a marathon without showing me he could run one mile first.

You will have stars who amaze you by running a marathon, asking seventeen people and receiving 15 gifts, but make sure they can run with five cards first.

Now here's the secret to getting your volunteers 20% of the way to their solicitation goal: make their own cards one of their five prospect cards.

Here's why. In Chip Heath and Dan Heath's book, *Switch: How to Change Things When Change is Hard* (p. 126), they tell the story of the local car wash that tested two different promotions featuring loyalty cards. One set of customers received a card with room for eight stamps. Each time they washed their car, they received a stamp, and with eight stamps, they earned a free car wash.

Another set of customers were given a loyalty card with space for ten stamps, with two stamps already on the card; i.e. customers still had to wash their vehicle eight times to earn a free car wash.

What do you think happened?

Only 19 percent of the customers receiving the eight-stamp card earned a free car wash, while 34 percent of those who received the ten-stamp card with the two stamps already in place earned a free char wash. And in fact, the second set of customers earned the free wash more quickly.

Why?

Because the customers who received the ten-stamp card with the two stamps already in place were immediately 20 percent of the way to their goal of a free car wash.

When you make the solicitor's prospect card part of their five cards, as soon as they fill it out, they are twenty percent of the way to their goal of asking five people to give to the campaign. You have helped each volunteer to create momentum by making twenty percent of their goal on the day of the kickoff.

GREEN LIGHT
FUNDRAISING

Setting the agenda for the advance gifts kickoff

You have overseen the recruiting of a top notch group of community and business leaders for your advance gifts phase. You need to honor their time during the kickoff by having a printed agenda for everyone to ensure all the essential topics are covered and to ensure that the time flows efficiently and effectively.

Here is a sample agenda for an advance gifts kickoff with comments in italics:

1. Welcome and introductions by advance gifts campaign chairperson (2-3 minutes)

   Comment: A number of people will be speaking at the kickoff. Talk to each speaker ahead of time so that they know exactly what is expected of them in terms of content and time. Put the time allotted for each person in parentheses to help the flow of the meeting. Your goal is to complete the kickoff in 45-60 minutes.

   The advance gifts chairperson welcomes everyone to the kickoff meeting and oversees the introductions of team captains, team members, and staff; lastly, and most importantly, the advance gifts chairperson introduces the campaign chairperson and invites the chairperson to speak to the group.

2. Greetings from campaign chairperson (2-3 minutes)

   Comment: Key topics to be covered by chairperson: Thank advance gifts chairperson and team for volunteering; why he/she volunteered to be the campaign chairperson; the importance that the advance gifts play in the campaign—1) 60% to 70% of the campaign goal by securing gifts in the range of (insert advance gifts range) 2) building incredible momentum for the completion of the campaign through the special gifts phase; thank each person for volunteering; introduce the executive director to tell volunteers more about the work of the organization.

Need More Help From Rich? See p. 241

GREEN LIGHT FUNDRAISING

3. Executive director on how the nonprofit transforms lives (7 minutes)

   Comment: Thank advance gifts team for volunteering: tell a dramatic story that highlights the work of the nonprofit in transforming lives through one of its programs; at the end of the story, the executive director should highlight how many other people benefit from the same program; briefly describe whom the organization serves, including number of people and the geographic area served; describe how essential the sustainable fundraising campaign is to the nonprofit's work of transforming lives; tell a second dramatic story that highlights the work of the nonprofit in transforming lives through one of its programs--highlight how many other people benefit from the same program; thank the volunteers again; introduce the director of development, who will train the volunteers in the GOOD way of asking for a gift.

4. The GOOD Way of Asking for the Gift by director of development (10-12 minutes)

   (See Chapter 16 for the content for training "The GOOD Way of Asking for the Gift.")

5. Each volunteer picks five hot prospect cards. (10 minutes)

   Comment: Chapter 14 outlines the process for developing a list of advance gifts prospects. Here is a script that you may find helpful in giving your volunteers instructions for picking out five hot prospect cards:

   a. Pick five hot prospects. Your next step is to pick cards for five hot prospects. Hot prospects are people whom you know, have a relationship with, and and with whom you can be confident that you can secure a face to face meeting and successfully ask for a gift.

      The first step in selecting five hot prospects is to open your packet and take out your own prospect card. Take a look at the prospect card to see if you have any questions about how to fill it out, since we want you to be able to answer any questions your prospects may have. Any questions? (Pause)

      You are your first hot prospect. (Pause for laughter). As we mentioned in the training on the GOOD way to ask for a gift, the first step is to

GREEN LIGHT
FUNDRAISING

give generously yourself. Take a moment to fill out your prospect card (pause while they fill out the card). Then announce, "You are now twenty percent of the way to meeting your goal of asking five people for a gift to the campaign...plus, you were 100% successful in your first ask." (Pause for laughter).

b. Mark four on advance gifts prospect list. Look through the advance gifts prospects list in your packet and quickly mark the four people for whom you want prospect cards.

c. Adding names. If you have a friend whom you want to ask who is not on the list, check to see if the name is on the special gifts list. If the person is on the special gifts list, but you are confident you can ask for an advance gift, talk to the development assistant who will create a prospect card for your friend.

d. Pick up your cards. Once you have marked the four names on your prospect list, go to the table and pick up the cards.

e. Two people going for the same card. If more than one person wants the same prospect card, negotiate.

f. Record cards with the development assistant. Once you have your four additional cards, show them to the development assistant who will mark the names of your four prospects on the master list so that we can track who has which cards.

g. Want to be a star? Take your additional four cards now. If, after you have completed asking your five people and they've each said yes or no, you want more prospect cards, contact me. We'd be happy to give you five more cards, because you are a star.

h. Reporting to your captain. A word on reporting your progress to your captain. Each Friday morning, the advance gifts chairperson and captains will meet (in person or by conference call) with the development staff to talk over any issues that have arisen, and also to report on the progress. By Thursday evening of each week, report to your captain your progress—both yeses and nos. If you have a prospect card filled out with a gift, report the amount to your captain. On Friday morning, the captains will report the progress to the advance gifts chairperson and development staff.

Need More Help From Rich? See p. 241

GREEN LIGHT
FUNDRAISING

i. Complete the "Successful Ask Check List" for each potential donor with whom you meet. Each six-question checklist should take less than two minutes to complete and will give us valuable information on how effective our training was. At the same time, turn in all your gift cards in to your captain and turn in a completed checklist for each prospect you met with. You will find five "Successful Ask Check Lists" in your packet. If you need extra checklist, you can get them from our development assistant.

j. Advance gifts team score card. You'll also see in your packet a sample advance gifts team score card. Just like a basketball team keeps stats on its players to recognize the contributions of each team member, we'll be keeping stats to recognize each of your contributions to the campaign. (Point out the stats that the development office will be keeping). Highlight the awards that you and the advance gifts chairperson have agreed will be given in recognition of top producers in the advance gifts phase.

k. E-mail updates. Each Friday afternoon you'll get an e-mail from your friends in the development office that includes a progress report on the advance gifts phase.

l. Any questions? Select your four additional cards and record them with our development assistant. You can also turn in your personal prospect card and payment, if possible, to the assistant. The development assistant will then give you a "Successful Ask Check List" for each potential donor for whom you take a card.

You can find the script template with instructions for selecting five prospect cards in a Word document on the Green Light Fundraising website at http://greenlightfundraising.org/downloads/script.doc. Feel free to modify it to your style and circumstances.

In preparing for the advance gifts kickoff, remember what Alexander Clark said: "Let us watch well our beginnings, and results will manage themselves."

You can find a sample Advance Gifts Kickoff Agenda as a free download on the Green Light Fundraising website at http://greenlightfundraising.org/downloads/advance-agenda.doc

GREEN LIGHT
FUNDRAISING

Special Gifts Kickoff or Launching the Phase that Puts You over the Top

While the advance gifts phase builds momentum and raises the bulk of the funds in your sustainable fundraising campaign, it's the special gifts phase that will put you over the top.

The special gifts phase is the largest phase of the campaign in terms of the number of volunteers and the number of prospects.

Up until now, you have been quietly building towards this phase. You've secured the lead gift. You've spent a lot of time recruiting campaign leaders and volunteers for both the advance gifts and special gifts phases. You've quietly and powerfully raised 60%-80% of your campaign goal between the lead gift and the advance gifts commitments.

Now you are ready for the most exciting and most public phase of the campaign—the special gifts phase. Not only do you kickoff the phase with the largest number of volunteers but you kickoff a week long media blitz to tell the story of your nonprofit and your campaign.

In chapter nine we focused on developing a marketing plan with the goal of making it possible for potential special gifts donors to hear three times about your organization and the campaign during this week. When your special gifts volunteers call up their prospects, your goal is that the prospect will be aware of your organization and the campaign when they receive the call.

Your public relations blitz lays the groundwork for your special gifts volunteers to ask for the gifts that put your campaign over the top.

To plan for the special gifts kickoff, create packets as you did for the advance gifts kickoff, and use a similar format and agenda to the one that you used for the advance gifts kickoff.

Orient Volunteers to the Online Donate Button

Some of your donors, especially people who are giving in the special gifts phase, may prefer to donate online. As more people do business online, they are becoming more comfortable with making online donations. This is especially true of younger people. My son-in-law manages his and my daughter's finances and he pays every bill possible online. He and my daughter pledged $1,000 to underwrite this book and made their donations online.

Need More Help From Rich? See p. 241

GREEN LIGHT
FUNDRAISING

If your nonprofit has a website, it most likely has a donate button that allows people to give directly from their bank account or through their credit card.

You should orient your volunteers to the use of the donate button. Keep in mind that online services charge a fee of 2.5% to 3% for processing a payment.

Orient your volunteers, because at least some of the potential donors they approach will appreciate the convenience of online donations.

Make sure that the donation card includes the web address for your donate button for your donors who prefer to give online.

The finish line is in sight

When my daughter, Hannah, was in college, she ran cross-country and track for North Park University in Chicago. One day, she and other runners from North Park volunteered at the Chicago Marathon. She was stationed near the finish line and she was captivated as she watched the exhausted and exhilarated runners cross the finish line. Later that day she called me, very excited, and said, "I'm going to run a marathon."

A few years later, she and a friend ran together in the Flying Pig Marathon in Cincinnati, Ohio. We were at the starting line when several thousand runners started the race. The wonderful thing about a marathon is that very few people enter the race with the goal of winning. Most set a time goal or a goal to finish the race. Hannah set a goal of completing the race in 4:00 hours.

Even at the 20 mile marker, Hannah was looking chipper. But then the race began to take its toll. At the time she was going to college in a flat part of Indiana where she trained. However, the Flying Pig Marathon has a number of hills. The closer she got to the finish line the more her legs screamed from doing the hills. But she pressed on and finished the 26.4 mile race at 4 hours, 1 minute and 22 seconds.

Directing a sustainable fundraising campaign is a lot like running a marathon. Hannah trained for and planned her marathon run. To make her goal of running the marathon in four hours, she had to average each mile in nine minutes and nine seconds. But the unexpected happened those long, fierce hills that she had not included in her planning. The unexpected will happen in your campaign. Your task is to keep the campaign moving.

GREEN LIGHT
FUNDRAISING

Once you kickoff the special gifts phase, you are in the final few miles of the marathon. You may be tired and you may be discouraged, because almost certainly something has gone amiss in your first sustainable campaign. But you are also close to the finish line. Keep moving. Keep in touch with your special gifts chairperson, keep sending your weekly progress reports, and keep trouble shooting with the issues that arise. You have a date for the celebration of the success of the campaign. Keep moving. The finish line is in sight.

Looking ahead

Now that you know how to do kickoffs, you have one segment of donors that you still need to plan to reach—the smaller donors. You want to give them the opportunity to participate in transforming lives, and you can do that in two ways—a direct mail appeal or a special event. The next chapter will guide you in planning how to reach your small donors in a cost-effective way.

How can we improve?

E-mail us at (comment@greenlightfundraising.org) to let us know when something is unclear, or you have a suggestion for improving the book. Please identify the page and paragraph that needs improving.

Need More Help From Rich? See p. 241
GREEN LIGHT
FUNDRAISING

CHAPTER 18

Reaching The Salt Of The Earth: Your Smaller
Donors

As I mentioned earlier, my first fundraising job, was with Horizon House of Illinois Valley, Inc., a community organization that was fifteen years old and had done little fundraising.

Since by nature I love starting things, I was fortunate, along with a colleague, to be able to develop from the ground up a fundraising program. And since I am a writer, I naturally began thinking of starting with a direct mail appeal.

But before launching the appeal, I looked at what other nonprofits were doing in our area. That's when I realized that we had an incredible opportunity—we could "own" December. No other nonprofit had a highly-visible holiday giving program in the communities we served.

I began to ponder how we could combine a highly-visible holiday presence with a direct mail appeal. Since our nonprofit was situated on a high traffic corner, we decided to put up a large Christmas tree on the lawn close to the road and call the event the Tree of Hope.

For every $50 received, we added a light bulb to the tree. We launched the Tree of Hope with a media blitz on December 1, 1983, and on the same day we mailed a Christmas card appeal to every household in the five communities we served. As gifts came in, from the bottom up we lit the Tree of Hope.

Since then, Horizon House has "owned" December through the Tree of Hope, the first and most visible holiday fundraising program in the five communities served by the nonprofit.

Years later, when House adopted the Green Light Fundraising model, they continued the Tree of Hope appeal because it was an ideal way to reach smaller donors.

Two notes of caution

One, do not design a special event that is targeted at the same people who will be approached for advance or special gifts. Design the event to attract smaller donors.

Two, do not recruit a volunteer who is working in the advance and special gifts. You want your volunteers for advance gifts and special gifts to devote all of their volunteer energy to raising the bulk of the funds for your campaign.

Need More Help From Rich? See p. 241

GREEN LIGHT FUNDRAISING

A dash of salt through special events and fundraising letters

In designing your sustainable fundraising campaign, you need to plan to reach your smaller donors who can provide up to 20% of your goal.

The most effective way to reach smaller donors is through a special event and/or a direct mail appeal. Unless you already have a good mailing list, a special event will likely help you to reach small donors more effectively.

Special events

If you are an organization transitioning to Green Light Fundraising, you may already have a special event in place that can reach smaller donors. In that case, you can incorporate that event into your plan for the year.

One organization that I worked with, Youth Service Bureau Of Illinois Valley, was a youth organization that ran after-school programs, a day care, and programs for troubled youths and their families. They arranged for the children in several of their programs to paint abstract oil paintings on large canvases, and then held an art auction where people bought a ticket to attend the event and then bid on each piece of artwork.

I was especially impressed by the art auction special event, because it combined their mission—serving youths—with fundraising.

8 tips for organizing a great special event

1. Set the financial goal for your event.

   In determining what special event fits your organization the best, you need to set the financial goal. Remember, between your direct mail appeal and your special event, you want to raise up to 20% of your Green Light Fundraising goal.

   Once you set the financial goal for your special event, you can begin to consider the types of events that can help you reach the goal.

GREEN LIGHT
FUNDRAISING

2. Define the target market for your event.

You've already narrowed the possibilities of your target market because you are eliminating those members of your community who are being asked to give through the advance and special gifts phases. That means you have probably eliminated golf tournaments and galas which target higher-end donors.

Since you want your special event to succeed, it works best to target people in an existing segment of the community who already enjoy the activity that will be the focus of your event. By targeting an existing segment, you make it easier to get the word out for your special event, since people who are into similar sports or hobbies usually have their own networks.

Segments in your community that include smaller donors might be bowlers or other sports enthusiasts who play softball or basketball or enjoy long distance running or sport fishing. Other segments might include spaghetti dinner lovers, trivia buffs, or dancers to Sixties or Eighties music.

The next two tips will help you define your target market.

3. Look at your community.

Since special events tend to be the fundraiser of choice for many smaller nonprofits, market research will be readily available. Check newspapers to see what events are being promoted. Check online calendars of events in your community. Call other nonprofits and ask them how much they made on a special event. They may not tell you but then again they may.

When considering a special event, research other events in your community that appeal to smaller donors and tend to raise the amount of money you have set for a goal. Perhaps a nonprofit in your community has a great event that they do in the spring and no one is doing it in the fall.

Look at your community and look for opportunities. Opportunities can be found in new types of events, new target audiences, and for a new time of year for an old event.

GREEN LIGHT
FUNDRAISING

4. Look beyond your community.

Another good way to discover an opportunity for creating a unique special event in your community is to look at special events that are being done in other communities but not yours. You are looking for a special event that targets smaller donors and has the potential to raise sufficient funds to meet your goal for the event.

5. Recruit a champion.

As a development director or executive director, your goal is to invest as little time as possible in the special event. You and your executive director need to invest 90% of your time with the other phases of your campaign that provide 90% of the income.

The secret to raising money through a special event, while not letting it swallow too much time, is to recruit a champion from the community. The ideal is to have the champion, and a few of her friends, organize and run the event.

The champion may be a board member, or someone else with a connection to your organization and a passion for a specific type of event.

There are likely to be people in your community who love to put on events for charity. I worked with one organization that was approached by a couple of women who loved putting on Taco Nights. We agreed to let them put on Taco Night for our organization and they amazed us be raising over $7000 by selling tacos one evening. The only investment on the part of the organization was a bit of publicity.

6. Highlight your mission at the event.

A special event fundraiser is more than raising money. A unique experience is an essential part of the appeal of many special events. Perhaps people have a chance to meet a celebrity, enjoy a sport, or dress like they did in the 1970's. These are the appeals of special events.

GREEN LIGHT
FUNDRAISING

The challenge for nonprofits is to find creative ways to highlight their mission as part of a special event. Since special events vary tremendously, there's no recipe for the one right way to highlight your mission at an event. At one event, someone from your nonprofit may be able to speak for a couple of minutes. At another event, you might be able to set up a video on a loop that highlight your nonprofit and its mission or, you might set up a booth with printed materials and someone to engage in conversations with participants about your nonprofit and its mission.

Whatever the event, make sure that you design a way to highlight the mission of your organization.

7. Get names.

In all likelihood, the special event is going to attract people who have not had a previous connection with your nonprofit. This is a great opportunity to build the number of names on your donor software.

When designing your event, if possible, have people register ahead of time and collect names, addresses, and e-mail addresses. You want this information to add to your donor software, because you can use these names for direct mail appeals.

If you hold an event that does not require registration, like a pancake breakfast, hold a drawing for a $100 gift certificate or other item that your participants will be glad to sign up for the chance to win. Create a small form for the drawing and collect each person's name, address, phone number and e-mail address.

8. Create a scorecard for your special event.

When my son played organized basketball starting in sixth grade, I quickly learned the value of keeping a scorecard with keys stats like shots attempted, shots made, turnovers, assists, fouls, etc. Before I kept any stats, he tended to focus on any of his shortcomings in the game.

Once he knew I was keeping stats, he knew that we would look at his play and the play of his teammates more objectively, because he knew that they were being measured by more than the final score.

Need More Help From Rich? See p. 241

GREEN LIGHT
FUNDRAISING

Your special event volunteer leaders will appreciate having a scorecard and knowing by what stats they will be measured. Work with your volunteer leaders to set goals for each of the measurements. Here are some goals you may want to include on your sports card:

- Number of tickets sold
- Amount raised through ticket sales
- Number of sponsors
- Amount raised through sponsors
- Number of mentions in the press

Depending on the event, there may be other goals you want to measure.

The biggest advantage of having an agreed -upon set of goals for your special event scorecard is that it makes post-event evaluation easy and less emotional. Also, when your special event committee comes through with a great score, you have a great reason to celebrate.

Resources for Fundraising through Special Events

Fundraising Manual: A Step by Step Guide to Creating the Perfect Event by Micki Gordon.

Charity Village web site, at http://www.charityvillage.com, provides information including fundraising marketing, special events, and promotions on the library portion of the site.

Event Fundraising blog, at http://www.event360.com/blog. This blog is written by the Event 360 Team. Event 360 is the nation's leading designer and director of events for nonprofits. Event 360 engages hearts and minds through entertaining, moving, and flawless experiences that help nonprofits inspire record levels of interest, giving and loyalty.

GREEN LIGHT
FUNDRAISING

GrassrootsFundraising.org web site, at http://www.grassrootsfundraising.org, provides articles on a variety of fundraising issues, including special events. When you subscribe to Grassroots Fundraising Journal, you get unlimited access to their online archives.

The Nonprofit Good Practice Guide of the Dorothy A. Johnson Center for Philanthropy and Nonprofit Leadership, at http://www.nonprofitbasics.org, offers a resource directory and learning tool with nine topic areas, including fundraising and financial sustainability. To find resources on special events, select "nonprofit" in the search box and then search for "special events."

Reaching Your Smaller Donors through Direct Mail

My father is 86 and he gets a lot of fundraising letters. But, since he lives in a rural area, almost none of them are from local nonprofits. National nonprofits have traditionally done a lot of fundraising and prospecting through the mail because it's a cost-effective way to acquire new donors and to raise money from geographically-dispersed small donors.

As a local nonprofit, you have an advantage. You are local, which sets you apart from all the national mailers.

Direct mail fundraising is a specialized field of knowledge with lots of resources available to help you learn to raise funds effectively through letters. There are also consulting firms who specialize in doing direct mail fundraising for nonprofits. Few local nonprofits will have a large enough direct mail program to warrant hiring a consultant to do their direct mail program.

Still, if you include direct mail as a small piece of your Green Light Fundraising, you want to do it well enough to make your organization proud of your efforts and to make your direct mail appeal effective. I have opened many direct mail appeals from local nonprofits that made me shudder, because it was instantly obvious to me that the leaders of the nonprofit didn't know the basics of direct mail fundraising.

Don't make me shudder when I read your direct mail appeal.

In the tips below, we cover the essentials of direct mail. Following the tips is a list of resources that will help you go into more depth.

Need More Help From Rich? See p. 241

GREEN LIGHT
FUNDRAISING

Twelve tips for writing a successful fundraising letter

1. Start with a good mailing list.

   What's a good mailing list? A good mailing list is made up of people who have already given to your organization. People who have given to you already are much more likely than strangers to respond to a direct mail appeal.

   Of course, if your organization is new and does not have a group of donors, then the primary purpose of your first foray into direct mail is to acquire donors. In this case, you may have to buy a mailing list for your community or a segment of your community from a list broker. As people donate, you will be building a good mailing list that will provide support for your nonprofit for many years.

   A note of caution: if you buy a list for your community or part of your community, be sure to eliminate the people who are on your advance and special gifts prospect lists. You don't want someone whom you are going to meet in person to ask for $2,500 to receive a letter and give you $25 before the face to face solicitation meeting.

2. The story is the heart of your letter

   In the process of writing a case statement for your campaign, you have already written the heart of your letter—a story of a life transformed by the work of your nonprofit, or the story of a life in need of transformation through the work of your organization.

   People want to give to your nonprofit because they want to be part of helping your nonprofit to transform lives. As we covered in chapter seven, stories are the most effective way to communicate to potential donors the challenges facing the people your nonprofits serve and how your nonprofits help those people transform their lives by overcoming those challenges.

   When you sit down to write your letter, review chapter seven. It covers great ways to translate your nonprofit's work into powerful words that move donors to support your cause.

GREEN LIGHT
FUNDRAISING

3. Beyond junk mail: Getting the envelope opened

We have all learned to try to recognize junk mail in an instant. Post offices have a waste basket right next to the mail boxes, and a lot of fundraising letters are promptly dropped into the waste basket.

The first challenge you face is getting your potential donors to open your envelope.

Sometimes mailers disguise their purpose and trick us into opening the envelope by eliminating their name on the envelope so that you will open the envelope to find out who sent you the letter. I don't know about you. but I don't like to be tricked into opening a junk mail envelope. I can't throw away such letters fast enough.

How do you get people to open your envelope without trickery? Start your story on the envelope. You might do it through a photo and a caption. You might do it by including half of the opening sentence of your letter. People love stories because they want to see what will happen next. Create suspense on your envelope, and you increase the likelihood that your potential donor will open the envelope to see what happens next.

And include your organization's name and return address on the envelope so that your potential donor knows instantly who is sending them a letter. Over time, you want your donors to see your name and return address and instantly open the letter because they know they will be treated to a moving story and know they will likely give to help your cause.

4. To read or not to read: The first sentence.

Once you've persuaded your potential reader to open your envelope, you want them to read the letter. People will decide whether or not to read what you've written based on your first sentence.

When I wrote my novel, *Jonas and Sally*, I rewrote the opening sentence and the opening scene twenty or more times, because I knew that readers were going to determine whether or not they were going to spend several hours reading the novel based on the opening sentence.

Need More Help From Rich? See p. 241

GREEN LIGHT
FUNDRAISING

The same is true of your fundraising letter. Your potential donor will decide whether to spend a few minutes reading your letter based on the first sentence. Revise your opening sentence until it is captivating.

What is a captivating sentence? It's one that is so intriguing and powerful that it pulls the reader into the letter to see what happens next.

5. Writing for skimmers.

No matter how captivating your first sentence is, some of your potential donors will decide they don't have the time to read the whole letter. But if you have done a great job with the envelope and the opening sentence, they will want to know more.

You can write your letter for those who will read it all and those who will skim. You want to make it possible for skimmers to glance through your letter and absorb the essence of your appeal through headlines, underlining or highlighting.

6. Photos.

The only thing more powerful than a story is a story and a photo. You can ratchet up the power of your appeal by combining the photo of the person helped by your nonprofit with the story of how their life was transformed.

In Chapter 5 we mentioned a quote by Mother Teresa: "If I look at the mass, I will never act. If I look at the one, I will." Your letter should focus on the story and photos of one person. You will be helping your potential donors act.

7. Ask and you will receive

The second most important part of the letter (after the story) is to ask the reader to donate. Ask early in your letter, after you've hooked the reader and then, depending on the length of the letter, ask at least two more times (more if you choose to write a long letter of several pages).

GREEN LIGHT
FUNDRAISING

Tie your ask to the story of a transformed life. In chapter seven we told the story of the Youth Service Bureau worker who worked with a family who lived in recreational vehicle in January with the furnace no longer working. The temperature was minus sixteen degrees Fahrenheit. The story portrays how fundraising helped to save the family. Here are two sample asks based on the story:

Your gift to the YSB of Illinois Valley will help a family like the one living in a camper whose furnace went out when it was sixteen degrees below zero.

Please consider making a gift today to YSB of Illinois Valley. They help families succeed in every season like the family living in a camper whose furnace went out when it was sixteen degrees below zero.

8. How much to ask for.

For smaller donors, I prefer to ask for a gift within a range. And I don't ask for a specific amount in the letter, but rather offer several size gifts as options on the reply card.

Another approach that I've used is to figure out how much it costs to serve the person in the story for a day, a half day, or an hour, or a half hour, Depending on the cost you can use that figure in the request.

Please consider making a gift today of $32 to YSB of Illinois Valley. Your gift will pay for an hour of YSB helping families like the family living in a camper whose furnace went out when it was sixteen degrees below zero.

Direct mail is probably the most studied approach to fundraising, since it's easy to control the elements in the direct mail package. You can change one item in the package and mail it to a segment of your donors and see if the change increases or decreases giving when compared to those who received the standard package.

One such study showed that including the following sentence at the end of the final ask in a letter actually increased giving:

Any size gift helps.

9. The second most read part of your letter.

Need More Help From Rich? See p. 241

GREEN LIGHT FUNDRAISING

After the first sentence, the second most read section of your letter is the signature and P.S. Include an ask in your P.S. because that increases the likelihood that it will be read.

10. Making giving easy with a reply card and reply envelope.

You want to make giving as easy as possible. Modify the gift card that you developed for the volunteers in the advance and special gifts phases to make it into a direct mail reply card. The key modification needs to be a series of gift options of the size you hope your smaller donors will make. For smaller donors you might consider giving options of:

_____$50   _____$25   _____$10   _____other

Online giving is increasing. It's a convenient way of giving that more and more donors appreciate. You may want to include on your reply card the web address for giving online to your nonprofit.

National nonprofits routinely use business reply envelopes. When a donor uses a business reply envelope, the nonprofit pays upon delivery and the cost is significantly higher than a first class stamp. To decrease costs, I've used an envelope with a small box printed where the stamp goes and in the box had printed "Your stamp helps too."

You may want to test a sample of your mailing to see if providing a business reply envelope increases giving significantly over the "Your stamp helps too" envelope to justify using a business reply envelope.

11. Prepare your thank you letter ahead of time.

Once you have mailed the piece, your assistant is going to be busy processing the gifts and mailing thank you notes. If you've written the thank you ahead of time, you can mail merge the names and addresses into the letter and personalize the thank you. When the executive director signs the thank you, she can add a hand-written note to the letters of donors she knows.

GREEN LIGHT
FUNDRAISING

12. Create a direct mail scorecard.

When you do a direct mail appeal, create a scorecard ahead of time to help evaluate how effective your appeal was. Key elements in the scorecard spreadsheet:

- number of pieces mailed

- number of gifts received

- percent of people who responded to the mailing

- total gift income

- amount spent on postage

- amount spent on offset printing and copying,

- amount spent on assembling the letters

- total expenses

- total income

- total income minus total expense equals net income

You can find a sample direct mail scorecard on the Green Light Fundraising website at http://greenlightfundraising.org/downloads/direct-mail.xls.

Resources for Direct Mail

Sharpe Tips, http://www.raisersharpe.com/blog/ Direct mail fundraising pointers from Alan Sharpe, CFRE, fundraising practitioner, author, trainer and speaker.

Contributions Magazine. http://www.contributionsmagazine.com/feature.html. Contributions Magazine is a free online magazine published six times a year. Click on the above link and it'll take you a 'How To' Library that includes a section on direct mail.

How to write a human interest story. http://www.fundraising123.org/article/how-write-human-interest-story While this blog post is not directly related to writing a fundraising appeal, it provides the essential steps to writing a compelling story.

GREEN LIGHT
FUNDRAISING

How To Write The Perfect Fundraising Letter. http://www.writeexpress.com/fundraising-letter.html In addition to tips on writing a fundraising letter, this site markets a software program that helps you write a fundraising letter. I haven't used the software but you may find it a helpful shortcut to writing a fundraising letter for your organization.

Looking ahead

As you've read this book, you've discovered that Green Light Fundraising is quite a journey, filled with interesting people, setbacks, celebrations and countless details. The journey may seem overwhelming at times but, in your role as director of sustainable fundraising, you want to make the journey fun and rewarding for you and all your companions. In the next chapter, we give tips on how to make it fun and keep it fun.

How can we improve?

E-mail us at (comment@greenlightfundraising.org) to let us know when something is unclear, or you have a suggestion for improving the book. Please identify the page and paragraph that needs improving.

GREEN LIGHT
FUNDRAISING

CHAPTER 19

How Can We Make The Journey Fun?

When you launch a sustainable fundraising campaign, you always have the end in mind—that moment when you can announce, "We have surpassed our goal."

And yet, since Green Light Fundraising is a long journey, learning to enjoy each mile and each milestone along the way will make the journey more fun for all.

> It is good to have an end to journey towards; but it is the journey that matters in the end.
>
> - Ursula K. LeGuin

The fun question

Ask yourself and your various chairpersons, as you prepare for meetings and communicating about the campaign, "How can we make the journey fun?"

In his book, *Yours for the Asking: An Indispensable Guide to Fundraising and Management*, Reynold Levy, president of the Lincoln Center, asks, "Whenever we can communicate information in an amusing way that captures attention, why not?"

He gives an example. "One can place a Mostly Mozart Festival brochure in the board packet, or one can ask a staff member to dress head to toe as Mr. Mozart with powdered wig, and ask her to hand brochures to the delighted trustees as they come off the elevator on their way to the meeting."

Here's another example he gives. "One can announce that we have reached a critical milestone in our capital campaign of $500 million in pledges and support, or we can place at the seat of every trustee custom messages on M&Ms that mark the occasion."

Levy does an amazing job of involving volunteer leaders in the work of Lincoln Center. To do so, he makes sure that he is well prepared for every meeting, and he makes room for self-deprecating humor and fun. As he says of himself and his chairperson, we take "the work of the Lincoln Center more seriously than we take ourselves."

Some people have a talent for fun. By all means, tap into it. My colleague, Jack Domagall, had a quick wit and loved to think up ways of injecting fun into the routine of fundraising. It's common for community newspapers to shoot photos to promote charity events. Jack loved to think up wild and wacky photos to promote special events. Of course, the newspaper photographers always had fun working with him.

GREEN LIGHT
FUNDRAISING

For instance, one year, to promote our annual golf tournament, he lay down on the ground with a golf tee in his mouth and balanced a golf ball on the tee. A volunteer leader for the event stood beside him with a golf club, acting as if he was getting ready to tee off. Not only did the photographer have fun shooting the photo but it captured the attention of the newspaper readers also.

My wife and I once took a group of youths from our congregation to a national church youth convention. As everyone who's gone to a convention knows, announcements need to be made, even if most people tune them out. The organizers of this convention hired a couple of comedians to do the announcements. As strange as it may seem, the announcements were a highlight of the convention. You never knew what these two crazy guys would do during announcements.

Once, in the middle of the announcements, one of them announced he had to go to the restroom. His mike was still on as he flirted with a girl on the way to the restroom and then we were treated to the full sound effects.

Surely one of the conference organizers asked the fun question: "How can we make the announcements fun?"

You may be like me—not a comedian. I enjoy a good laugh at my own expense but my mind doesn't naturally think about how to make myself the center of a hilarious photo in the newspaper or how to turn announcement time into comedy time.

But, as executive director or development director, if you routinely ask, "How can we make this fun?" volunteer leaders and staff are likely to come up with great answers that can make your sustainable fundraising meetings and communications more enjoyable.

Ask the fun question, and you'll have miles of amusement as you raise an amazing amount of money to transform lives.

 Need More Help From Rich? See p. 241
GREEN LIGHT
FUNDRAISING

Six Fun Ways to Recognize, Celebrate and Honor Milestones and People

1. Gratitude is the foundation of celebration.

   As soon as we learn to talk, our parents teach us to say thank you when someone gives us something. A heartfelt thank you is a celebration of what another person has just given. Acknowledgments in person and through phone calls, notes, e-mails, and letters are great ways to recognize and honor volunteers and donors. "Thank you" should be your two most frequent words throughout the campaign.

2. Create your own Stanley Cup.

   The National Hockey League has the Stanley Cup, a trophy that the winner of the Stanley Cup playoffs keeps for a year until it travels with the next year's Stanley Cup winner. Originally inscribed the Dominion Hockey Challenge Cup, according to Wikipedia, the trophy was donated in 1892 by then Governor General of Canada, Lord Stanley of Preston, as an award for Canada's top-ranking amateur ice hockey club. In 1915, two professional hockey associations in Canada reached an agreement that they would play each other for the cup.

   A simple, yet unique way of recognizing your top performers, the people who bring in the most in gifts during each phase, is to create a version of the Stanley Cup for your nonprofit. Give the cup a unique name, perhaps named for your first campaign chairperson, and create a tradition of passing the cup from top performer to top performer each week. Encourage the winner to display the cup in their place of work for the week, and it will create many fun conversations.

3. Recruit a comedian.

   Take a page from the youth convention planners who hired a comedy duo to do the announcements. You may have someone on staff who has a talent for humor and may be the perfect person to do some of the routine announcements or training sections of your kickoffs. They'll be delighted to have their talent for humor recognized and used. Or, recruit a comedian from the community to enliven your kickoffs.

GREEN LIGHT
FUNDRAISING

4. Create friendly team competitions.

Some of your volunteers are likely to be competitive. You can create friendly competitions between advance gifts teams or between special gifts teams. Talk with the team leaders about the idea of giving an inexpensive, fun prize to the team that raises the most money. They are more likely to buy into it of they have a hand in designing the contest and choosing the prize. If the team leaders buy into it, you'll increase the fun factor in your campaign. Perhaps you want to create your version of the Stanley Cup and give it to the top-performing team each week, rather than the top performing individual. Each team member gets to keep the Cup for a day.

5. Dance on Wall Street in a grass skirt.

Sam Walton, founder of Wal-Mart, believed in working hard and having fun. In 1983 Walton promised his staff that he would dance down Wall Street in a grass skirt if Wal-Mart met its profit targets. Wal-Mart made its goal and Walton kept his promise, donning a grass skirt and Hawaiian shirt over his suit and dancing the hula in front of Merrill Lynch.

An executive director or campaign chairperson can inject fun into the campaign by making a promise of doing something silly in public if the campaign meets its goal. Of course, this only works if the executive director or campaign chairperson is comfortable with making and keeping wild promises.

6. Design unique recognition gifts.

A leader of a company once found a penny in the parking lot and spontaneously gave it to an employee who was doing a particularly good job. He was surprised to find out later that the employee prized the penny and displayed it on his desk. Picking up on the employee's reaction, he had pennies mounted on a small stand in clear plastic and handed them out to employees who were doing a great job.

Traditionally, nonprofits have given out plaques to honor volunteers. Ask the fun question: How can we create a fun alternative to a plaque that is unique to your nonprofit and will be treasured by our volunteers?

   Need More Help From Rich? See p. 241
GREEN LIGHT
FUNDRAISING

Success requires celebration

A successful campaign requires a lot of work by a lot of people—donors, volunteers and staff. Great efforts should naturally lead to great celebrations.

Part of the responsibility of the development staff is to work with the campaign chairperson to plan a campaign wrap-up celebration that fits with your nonprofit and your community. Options include:

- Formal dinner.

    United Way organizations often celebrate their campaign wrap-ups with a dinner where the top donors and volunteers are recognized.

- Hors d'oeuvres.

    A less formal and less expensive way to celebrate the wrap-up is an after-hours event with free hors d'oeuvres, soft drinks and a cash bar.

- Annual meeting.

    Some nonprofits have an annual meeting with a dinner to honor staff, volunteers and board members. Some nonprofits use this event to honor the campaign chairperson and the person who gave the lead gift to the campaign.

As you plan the wrap-up celebration, be sure to ask the fun question: How can we make this event enjoyable and memorable for the volunteers and top donors?

If you settle on a more formal event, script it tightly so that no speaker wanders off course and takes the whole event into a wasteland called boredom.

Honor thy staff

A Green Light Fundraising campaign is the primary work of your development staff each year. You deserve to celebrate together as well as work together. Plan a development staff celebration.

After the campaign is complete, and after you've hosted the wrap-up for volunteers and top donors, you may want to go out together for a long lunch, tell war stories, remember the funny moments of the campaign, and find your own special ways of giving thanks for being able to work together.

GREEN LIGHT
FUNDRAISING

During the campaign, you've worked together under pressure of one deadline after another. Honor your staff by finding a way to relax together and celebrate the amazing fete you've just pulled off—raising an amazing amount of money to transform the lives of the people with whom your nonprofit works.

Plan your own personal celebration

When I completed my first campaign, I was exhilarated and exhausted. I not only planned a wrap-up celebration, but I planned to leave immediately after the wrap-up celebration for my own celebration—a two-day personal retreat in Chicago.

I live on a farm, so my idea of getting away from it all is to head to the city. You'll have your own idea of a great way to get away and celebrate.

As a development director or executive director, you will pour yourself into the campaign, especially your first one when it will feel like uncharted territory. Plan your own personal time of celebration and renewal. If you celebrate and renew at the end of each campaign in a way that uniquely fits you, you'll be ready to start the journey all over again next year.

Looking ahead

Writing this book for you has been a long journey—27 years to learn fundraising and 18 months of raising the funds to underwrite the book, write the book, and rewrite it.

Now, when I asked myself the fun question, I decided to do my own wrap-up. In the next chapter, I do my personal thanks to the people who have had a hand in helping me write this book.

How can we improve?

E-mail us at (comment@greenlightfundraising.org) to let us know when something is unclear, or you have a suggestion for improving the book. Please identify the page and paragraph that needs improving.

 Need More Help From Rich? See p. 241  GREEN LIGHT FUNDRAISING

CHAPTER 20

A Word Of Personal Thanks

During the six months I wrote the first draft of this book, I went through a series of medical setbacks that made writing this book both a challenge and a gift.

In the fall of 2009, I was raising the funds to underwrite this book when I suffered five compression fractures in my back, as well as a series of lung infections. When it became apparent that I could no longer travel to raise the funds, I switched gears and focused on writing the book, trusting that when I finished the book, I would be able to complete raising the funds to design the book and the website that will make this book an invaluable tool for fundraisers like you.

Writing this book was an exercise in remembering and dreaming. As I wrote, I remembered the mentors, donors, volunteers, colleagues, and clients who taught me all that went into creating this Green Light Fundraising system.

I've also been dreaming of you, the nonprofit leaders in need of a good fundraising system to sustain your organization. I've been dreaming of your excitement as you discover this system, apply it, improve it, and raise more money than you thought possible.

I've been dreaming of hearing stories from you of the lives that have been transformed by the work of your organization, the lives that have been given a green light through your fundraising. Thank you ahead of time for all the good work you will do as you learn and apply Green Light Fundraising.

I can't thank every mentor, donor, volunteer, colleague, and client who has shaped this book, but there are a few names that move me every time I think of them.

Allan Howe. (retired).

You've been a friend for many years, and when I approached you about being the chairperson of our Green Light Fundraising campaign, you not only said yes but gave generously and joined me in meeting with our top prospects.

Deborah Schmidt. Chief Operating Officer, Toji Trading Group.

You were the first person we asked for the lead gift of $5,000 for this project. You are a true leader and said yes. I still remember the joy I felt. Thanks for believing in this project and making this book possible for the nonprofit community.

Need More Help From Rich? See p. 241

GREEN LIGHT FUNDRAISING

Jim Monterastelli, CEO, Horizon House of Illinois Valley, Inc.

You said yes after I handed you a job description in 1983 for a new position for me, development director. And then, for the next 15 years, you were a great boss. I was truly blessed to work for you and the people served by HHIV.

Jack Domagall. (Deceased)

Jack, I had the privilege of working with you and being a friend for 25 years. What a fundraising team we made. I miss you.

Frank Koob. (Deceased)

You were a donor, but much more than a donor. You gave me much support and encouragement when I first launched a planned giving program. Later, when we launched our first sustainable fundraising campaign you gave the lead gift. Always you taught me, through your stories from your careers in everything from engineering to owning a Ford dealership to starting the first Christmas tree farm in Illinois.

Bill Glenn. Retired YMCA executive

You generously taught me how to do a capital campaign, and taught me many of the principles on which Green Light Fundraising is based. Because you generously gave your time and wisdom, we raised the money to transform the lives of over 70 people, moving them from a nursing home into small group homes.

Dee Anderson. (Retired)

You were the assistant director in the first capital campaign I directed. You taught me that fundraising is in the details, in doing things right, and in connecting deeply with volunteers.

Dave McClure. Executive Director, Youth Service Bureau of Illinois Valley.

You were the first client with whom I tested many of these ideas. Thank you for generously letting me use the stories from your organization in the book. You were the ideal client, doing great work and being eager to learn how to do sustainable fundraising.

GREEN LIGHT
FUNDRAISING

Robert and Grayce Mitchell, Administrative Partner at K & L Gates law firm and the Service Learning Coordinator for Ballard High School.

We have been good friends since we first met at the University of North Dakota in the early 1970's. In the last few years, you have generously supported several Evergreen Leaders projects. Thanks.

Plow Creek Fellowship (past and present members)

It's been an honor to share life with you for the past 33 years as an intentional Christian community. We've shared this farm, a mission, and deep friendships. Thanks.

Evergreen Leaders board, past and present. (Leonide Begly, Andy Fitz, Tom Fleming, Stephanie Grimes, Jason Harrison, Tutuk Horning, Marvin Porter, Lynn Reha, Edward Sims, Tim Stair, Anne Stewart).

What a journey we have been on since the first board met Memorial Day weekend in 2003. You supported me and prodded me as a board should. Thanks for making this book possible.

Sarah Foss. (wife, RN, mother to our three children)

I saved the best for last. You have been with me on this long and crazy 27-year journey as I learned to be a fundraiser and now as I begin to teach fundraising to others. In the last six months, most of which I couldn't drive, you provided me with help in countless ways. You, as much as me, have made this book--this gift to the nonprofit community--possible. Thanks beyond words, my love.

Need More Help From Rich? See p. 241

GREEN LIGHT
FUNDRAISING

Special thanks to those who gave me feedback on the manuscript for this book

This book was much improved by the work of those who read the manuscript and gave me the feedback I needed to take to the next level. Thanks to:

- Elizabeth Longenecker, a great copy editor. Thanks for catching all my split infinitives and much more.

- Jessica Mason, a great line editor who pointed each time I started to get repetitious and much more.

- Carol Fesco, who has led sustainable fundraising campaigns for the last few years, and made great comments on the content; and

- Sarah Foss, who has been my editor ever since I asked you to read *Jonas and Sally* in the summer of 1993 and we both discovered your talent for editing.

Thanks to each of you. Any errors that remain are my responsibility and mine alone.

How can we improve?

Click on this e-mail address (comment@greenlightfundraising.org) to let us know when something is unclear, or you have a suggestion for improving the book. Please identify the page and paragraph that needs improving.

GREEN LIGHT
FUNDRAISING

Special thanks to the donors who underwrote this book

When you raise funds you develop a special bond with the people and businesses that support your work. I read the following names and I see old friends and new friends and my heart is filled with gratitude for each because these are the people who truly made this book possible.

Thank you

Lauren Baranco

Bob Betzelberger

Al and Ellen Butkus

Central Bank Illinois

Centrue Bank

Comprehensive Insurance Services, Inc.

Connecting Point Computer Centers

Senator Gary and Mrs. Debra Dahl

Dan and Nancy Fitzgerald

Tom and Kay Fleming

Jon Foss

Rich and Sarah Foss

Mike and Ginia Goggio

Donny and Hannah Hackworth

Jim Harnish

Bruce and Rachel Headings

Jim Heing and Associates

Wendell Hendershott

Linda Hoff and Jim Irvin

Allan and Jeanne Howe

Mitch and Ann Kingsley

Elvin Krabill, DDS

Brad and Sarah Lalk

Dave McClure

Miller Group Charitable Trust Fund

Rob and Grayce Mitchell

Jim and Vickie Monterastelli

Dave and Hope Salmon

Deborah Schmidt

Anne Sigler

Anne Stewart

Mark and Jocelyn Thornton

Devon Warwick

Woju and Heidi Worabo

Carol A Youngqist.

Looking ahead

Do you need more help with the sticky questions you have about Green Light Fundraising? The next section, you'll find how to join the Green Light Fundraising Club, an affordable way to get all your questions answered.

GREEN LIGHT FUNDRAISING

NEED PERSONAL HELP FROM RICH TO DO GREEN LIGHT FUNDRAISING?

The impetus for this book began when I kept running into nonprofits that could not afford our modest consulting fees ($115 an hour) and yet desperately needed to learn how to set up Green Light Fundraising systems to raise funds to transform lives.

I especially remember a small nonprofit that was setting up a university in a former war torn country in Africa and sometimes did not have the funds to pay their executive director, let alone a fundraising consultant.

They needed desperately a sustainable fundraising system to sustain their organization while getting the university off the ground, and yet they couldn't afford it.

From the beginning, we planned to give a version of this book away as a free ebook as a way to make it possible for more nonprofits to do Green Light Fundraising.

We want you and your nonprofit to thrive.

Still, as I was planning the book, I kept having a nagging question: What about nonprofit executive directors and development directors who will have questions about how to do Green Light Fundraising within their unique situation?

About ¾ of the way through writing the first draft of this book, I found the answer.

I joined Robert Middleton's Action Plan Marketing Club to learn how to get the message out about this ebook. As I began using the services of the Action Plan Marketing Club, I realized that it was the powerful, low-cost model that I was looking for to support people like you as you apply the principles and best practices of Green Light Fundraising to your nonprofit.

Free stuff

The Green Light Fundraising website, http://greenlightfundraising.org/, has a blog plus other free articles that can help you grow your expertise as a sustainable fundraiser.

In addition, go to http://greenlightfundraising.org/glfr-subscription/ to sign up for the Green Light Fundraising e-letter that will deliver short, powerful sustainable fundraising tips and tools to your inbox every other week.

 Need More Help From Rich? See p. 241

Low Cost Help

We've created the Green Light Fundraising Club as a low cost way for you to find ongoing help while you learn sustainable fundraising.

For a fee of $29 a month, you can sign up for the Green Light Fundraising Club. As a special offer to readers of Green Light Fundraising, you can go to (http://greenlightfundraising.org/glfr-club/) to try out the Green Light Fundraising Club for one month for 99¢.

Sign up today and you will gain access to the Club membership section of our website that provides you with additional resources. The Green Light Fundraising Club will provide you access to:

- The Green Light Fundraising leadership modules;
- Coaching calls with Rich covering all aspects of sustainable fundraising where you can ask your sustainable fundraising questions
- Expert interviews on specific issues in sustainable fundraising
- Podcasts of coaching calls and expert interviews

Video tutorials on key parts of sustainable fundraisingNonprofits need to use their funds wisely and that is why we make it possible for you to test drive the Club for a month for $0.99. The second month you pay $29 and you can quit anytime.

Join us today and you will have the green light to develop your nonprofit's sustainable fundraising.

GREEN LIGHT
FUNDRAISING

Rich Foss' Bio

Rich has spent over 27 years raising funds as a development staff member and consultant. He has a passion for helping community nonprofits raise funds to transform lives. He co-founded Evergreen Leaders, a nonprofit, in 2003 to help nonprofits thrive by giving ordinary people the tools to help their groups thrive. He has developed the 7 Paths as a way to teach and coach nonprofit leaders how to help their organizations thrive. In addition, he developed Green Light Fundraising, a sustainable fundraising system that helps nonprofits thrive by raising more funds every year. Since 1977, Rich and his wife, Sarah, have been part of Plow Creek Fellowship, an intentional Mennonite community located in rural Illinois. He enjoys fresh fruits and vegetables from early spring to late fall, grown by his friends who work on Plow Creek's farm. He and his wife, Sarah, delight in their three children, their children's spouses, and their four grandchildren. He is the author of the novel, *Jonas and Sally*.

Need More Help From Rich? See p. 241

GREEN LIGHT
FUNDRAISING